PERSONAL

An Elective Course in Journal Writing

Eric Kraft

Charles Neuschafer

Ginn and Company

A Xerox Education Company

Acknowledgments

Grateful acknowledgment is made to the following publishers, authors, and agents for permission to use copyrighted materials:

Addison-Wesley Publishing Company for the excerpt on page 157 by Gordon W. Allport, *The Nature of Prejudice,* 1954, Addison-Wesley, Reading, Mass. Used by permission.

Avon Books for "Springtime Study Hall Blues" and "The Walls Belong to the People." Reprinted from *How Old Will You Be in 1984?,* edited by Diane Divoky, by arrangement with Avon Books. Copyright © 1969 by Avon Books. Used by permission.

The Helen Brann Literary Agency for "Two Guys Get Out of a Car" by Richard Brautigan on page 62. Copyright © 1971 by Richard Brautigan. Reprinted with permission of the Helen Brann Literary Agency.

City Lights Books for the poem "Birthplace Revisited" from *Gasoline* by Gregory Corso. Copyright © 1958 by Gregory Corso. Reprinted by permission of City Lights Books. Also for the excerpt "Here Is Someone . . ." on page 139 from *Antonin Artaud Anthology* edited by Jack Hirschman. Copyright © 1965 by City Lights Books. Reprinted by permission of City Lights Books.

The Dial Press for the excerpt on page 180, from "Previous Condition," copyright 1948 by James Baldwin, from the book, *Going to Meet the Man* by James Baldwin. Reprinted by permission of the publisher, The Dial Press. Originally appeared in *Commentary.* Also for the excerpts on pages 83 and 134 from *Coming of Age in Mississippi* by Anne Moody. Used by permission.

Doubleday & Company, Inc. for the excerpt on pages 8 and 9, from *Paul Bunyan and His Great Blue Ox* by Wallace Wadsworth, copyright 1926 by George H. Doran Company. Reprinted by permission of Doubleday & Company, Inc. Also for the excerpt on page 50. Copyright 1919 by Sun Printing & Publishing Association, "Archy gets restless again" from *Archy Does His Part* from the book *The Lives and Times of Archy and Mehitabel* by Don Marquis. Reprinted by permission of Doubleday & Company, Inc. Also for the telegram on page 66 and "Them Hors D'Oeuvres" both from *The Mason Williams Reading Matter* copyright 1964, 1966, 1967, 1969 by Mason Williams. Reprinted by permission of Doubleday & Company, Inc. Also for the excerpt on page 70 from *The Silent Language* copyright © 1959 by Edward T. Hall. Reprinted by permission of Doubleday & Company, Inc. Also for the excerpt on page 80 from *Journeys Out of the Body* copyright © 1971 by Robert A. Monroe. Reprinted by permission of Doubleday & Company, Inc. Also for the abridged excerpt on page 104 from *The Diary of a Young Girl* by Anne Frank, copyright 1952 by Otto H. Frank. Reprinted by permission of Doubleday &

Company, Inc. Also for the excerpt on page 108 from *The Story of My Life* by Helen Keller. Reprinted by permission of Doubleday & Company, Inc. Also for permission of Doubleday & Company, Inc. Also for "The Black Sheep" from *The Black Sheep and Other Fables* by Augusto Monterroso, translated by Walter I. Bradbury. Copyright © 1971 by Doubleday & Company, Inc. Reprinted by permission of publisher. Also for excerpts on page 160 by Arch Whitehouse from *Heroes and Legends of World War I* copyright © 1964 by Arch Whitehouse. Reprinted by permission of Doubleday & Company, Inc. Also for the excerpt on pages 163-164 from *The Private Diaries of Stendahl* edited by Robert Sage, Copyright 1954 by Robert Sage. Reprinted by permission of Doubleday & Company, Inc. Also for "Crossing Brooklyn Ferry" (on page 167) and excerpts from "Song of Myself" by Walt Whitman (on page 187) from *The Complete Poetry and Prose of Walt Whitman.* Reprinted by permission of Doubleday & Company, Inc.

Funk and Wagnalls Publishing Company, Inc., for excerpts on pages 128 and 129 from *How to Torture Your Mind* by Ralph L. Woods, Copyright © 1969 by Ralph L. Woods. With permission of Funk & Wagnalls Publishing Company, Inc., publishers.

Harcourt Brace Jovanovich, Inc., for the poem "Portrait of a Machine." Copyright, 1923, by Harcourt Brace Jovanovich, Inc.; copyright, 1951, by Louis Untermeyer. Reprinted from *Long Feud: Selected Poems* by Louis Untermeyer by permission of Harcourt Brace Jovanovich, Inc. Also for excerpts on pages 140, 162, and 187, from Leonard Woolf, from *A Writer's Diary, Being Extracts from the Diary of Virginia Woolf.* Used by permission of Harcourt Brace Jovanovich, Inc. Also for the poem "Phizzog" by Carl Sandburg. From *Good Morning, America,* copyright, 1928, 1956, by Carl Sandburg. Reprinted by permission of Harcourt Brace Jovanovich, Inc. Also for the excerpt on page 108 from Chapter 6 of *Biology and Man* by George Gaylord Simpson. Also for excerpts on pages 19, 22, 43, 85, and 108 from *The Notebooks of Leonardo da Vinci,* translated and edited by Edward MacCurdy. Reprinted by permission of the publisher.

Harper & Row, Publishers, Inc., for the excerpt on page 134. Excerpt from p. 43 ("From the beginning . . . the helmet off.") in *Paper Lion* by George Plimpton. Copyright © 1964, 1965, 1966 by George Plimpton. By permission of Harper & Row, Publishers, Inc. Also for the excerpt on page 144 from p.211 ("Do all of you . . . . . . rats with it.") in *A Choice of Weapons* by Gordon Parks. Copyright © 1965, 1966 by Gordon Parks. Reprinted by permission of Harper & Row, Publishers, Inc. Also for witticisms on pages 26 and 63 from pp. 82 and 400 of *The New Speaker's Treasury of Wit and Wisdom* by Herbert V. Prochnow. By permission of Harper & Row, Publishers, Inc. Also for the poem "Mirror" from *The Carpentered Hen and Other Tame Crea-*

tures by John Updike. Copyright © 1957 by John Updike. By permission of Harper & Row, Publishers, Inc. Also for the poem "Incident" from *On These I Stand* by Countee Cullen. Copyright 1925 by Harper & Row, Publishers, Inc. renewed 1953 by Ida M. Cullen. Also for the excerpt on page 166 from *Memoirs of a Dutiful Daughter* by Simone de Beauvoir. Harper Colophon Book. Used by permission of Harper & Row, Publishers. Also for the excerpt on page 120 from page 166 "April 21" from *Writing and Thinking on the Waterfront* by Eric Hoffer. Copyright © 1969 by Eric Hoffer. Also for the excerpt on page 64 from page 65 from *Letters from a Traveller* by Pierre Teilhard de Chardin. Copyright © 1962 in the English translation by William Collin's Sons & Co., Ltd., London, and Harper & Row, Publishers. Also for the excerpt on page 6 from pp. 223-224 from *Letters from the Earth* by Mark Twain. Copyright © 1962 by The Mark Twain Company. Also for excerpts on pages 88-89 and 4 from pp. 287-88 and 305-6 in *Mark Twain's Notebook* edited by Albert Bigelow Paine. Copyright 1935 by The Mark Twain Company. Also for the paragraph on page 142 from *Huckleberry Finn* by Mark Twain. Also for the excerpt on page 154 from *The Age of Discontinuity* by Peter F. Drucker. Reprinted by permission of Harper & Row, Publishers, Inc.

Holt, Rinehart and Winston, Inc., for the poem "Steam Shovel." From *Upper Pasture* by Charles Malam. Copyright 1930, © 1958 by Charles Malam. Reprinted by permission of Holt, Rinehart and Winston, Inc.

Little, Brown and Company for the excerpt on page 7. Copyright © 1967, 1968, 1969, 1970 by Little, Brown and Company. From *How to Talk Back to Your Television Set* by Nicholas Johnson, by permission of Atlantic-Little, Brown and Co. Also for the excerpt on page 177. Copyright ©, 1959, by Warren Miller. From *The Cool World* by Warren Miller, by permission of Little, Brown and Co. Also for the excerpt on page 11 from *Come Back, Dr. Caligari* by Donald Barthelme. Also for the excerpt on page 149 from *People in a Diary: A Memoir* by S. N. Berhman, originally published in *The New Yorker.* Also for the poems on pages 153 and 155 from *The Complete Poems of Emily Dickinson,* edited by Thomas H. Johnson. Used by permission of Little, Brown and Company.

The Macmillan Company for the illustration by Julian Leek on page 84. Reprinted with permission of The Macmillan Company from *Phrenology* by Sybil Leek. Copyright © 1970 by Sybil Leek. Also for twelve lines of "The Lake Isle of Innisfree." Reprinted with permission of The Macmillan Company from *Collected Poems* by William Butler Yeats. Copyright 1906 by The Macmillan Company, renewed 1935 by William Butler Yeats. Also for the poem "Little Things." Reprinted with permission of The Macmillan Company from *Collected Poems* by

iv

Introduction

To the Student:

Because an individual's journal—like an individual's life—is never exactly like anyone else's, it can be said that there are as many kinds of journals as there are people who keep and have kept them. People have kept journals that resemble scrapbooks, diaries, histories, travelogs, rogues' galleries, practice books, sketch pads, catalogs, or a combination of any of these. Yet all journals have one thing in common: each is a record of its author's encounters with life.

In a journal the writer can find a private place in which to record personal thoughts, feelings, impressions, experiences, and ideas in whatever form or style he or she wants. Entries can be written well or badly, roughly or in finished form, with only the writer as judge. In a journal the journal keeper can test wild ideas and can be angry, wise, sad, elated, and foolish. There the journal writer can preserve observations of life past and present, as well as speculations about the future.

Personal is a collection of materials that you are invited to read, think about, interpret, react to, and, in whatever way you choose, possibly write about in your own journal. Included are photographs, drawings, poems, song lyrics, excerpts from diaries and journals, odd bits and pieces of information, news clippings, puzzles, epigrams, magazine ads, and many suggestions to help you get your thoughts and feelings onto paper. Rather than an end in itself, the book is intended to be only a beginning for the personal thinking and writing you develop on your own.

The Authors

1

The true purpose of education is to help everyone fulfill himself as an individual.

"I don't know," I cried without being heard, "I do not know. If nobody comes, then nobody comes. I've done nobody any harm, nobody's done me any harm, but nobody will help me. A pack of nobodies. Yet that isn't all true. Only, that nobody helps me—a pack of nobodies would be rather fine, on the other hand. I'd love to go on an excursion—why not? —with a pack of nobodies. Into the mountains, of course, where else? How these nobodies jostle each other, all these lifted arms linked together, these numberless feet treading so close! Of course they are all in dress suits. We go so gaily, the wind blows through us and the gaps in our company. Our throats swell and are free in the mountains! It's a wonder that we don't burst into song."

Franz Kafka

He advised me to keep a journal of my life, fair and undisguised. He said it would be a very good exercise, and would yield me infinite satisfaction when the ideas were faded from my remembrance. I told him that I had done so ever since I left Scotland. He said he was very happy that I pursued so good a plan. . . . He said indeed that I should keep it private, and that I might surely have a friend who would burn it in case of my death. . . . I told Mr. Johnson that I put down all sorts of little incidents in it. "Sir," said he, "there is nothing too little for so little a creature as man. It is by studying little things that we attain the great knowledge of having as little misery and as much happiness as possible."

James Boswell
LONDON JOURNAL

It must be told that my second work day is a bust as far as getting into the writing. I suffer as always from the fear of putting down the first line. It is amazing the terrors, the magics, the prayers, the straightening shyness that assails one. It is as though the words were not only indelible but that they spread out like dye in water and color everything around them. A strange and mystic business, writing. Almost no progress has taken place since it was invented.

John Steinbeck
JOURNAL OF A NOVEL: THE EAST OF EDEN LETTERS

"Today was like a . . ."
Begin or end some of your journal entries by completing that statement.

journal n. (ME from OF *journal* daily from L *diurnal* diurnal) 1. a daily record, an account of experiences, observations, or events. . .

Find the best time to write your journal entry. Some writers feel they are at their best in the early hours of the morning, others late in the evening. What is your prime time?

Invent a correspondent, someone you can write to who really understands you. Write some entries as letters to this person. You may want to make most or all of your entries in the form of letters to this imaginary correspondent.

3

In the local movie theater, you can buy mint-flavored lozenges with the words: "Will you marry me one day?" "Do you love me?" written on them, together with the replies: "This evening," "A lot," etc. You pass them to the girl next to you, who replies in the same way. Lives become linked together by an exchange of mint lozenges.

Albert Camus
NOTEBOOKS, 1935–1942

More hugging and kissing by boys and girls and young men and maids in the streets at night and parks by day! And no chaffing them by anybody. I met a couple tonight, aged 17 and 14, a dozen times, around the garden. They ought to have done the blushing, but I presently found they could not be depended on, and had to do it myself.

Mark Twain
NOTEBOOK

An idea that strikes me is this: Every day we leave a part of ourselves behind us on the road. Everything around us disappears—faces, relatives, people who walk past in the street. The generations pass away in silence, everything falls and is gone, the world slips through our fingers, our illusions are shattered, we watch the ruin of everything. And, as if this were not enough, we fall into ruin ourselves. We are as alien to our earlier selves as if it were another person. I no longer know what I was a few years ago—my pleasures, my feelings, my thoughts. My body has passed away, my soul has passed away also, time has carried everything off. I am the evidence of my metamorphosis—I no longer know what I was. The things I enjoyed as a child I can no longer understand; my observations, my hopes, my creations as a young man are lost. What I have thought, what I have felt (my only precious possessions), the consciousness of my former existence, I possess no more: it is a past that has been swallowed up. . . . If a person remembered all that he had observed and learned in his life, he would be wise indeed.

definitely read

Henri Frédéric Amiel
PRIVATE JOURNAL *[adapted slightly]*

Do this

In ten years you will have forgotten most of the things that fill your daily life now. Try ensuring that you'll be able to recapture some of them. Try one of these:
☐**List the little things that characterize your surroundings.**
☐**Predict what your strongest memories of this time will be in ten years.**
☐**Predict what you will most easily forget.**

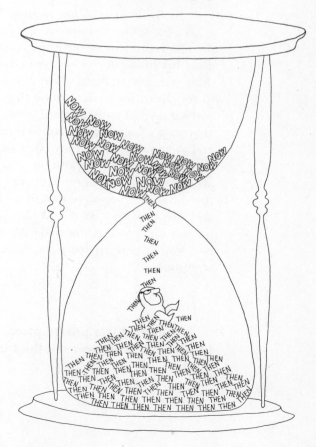

All of the animals except man know that the principal business of life is to enjoy it.

Samuel Butler

What situations in today's world make you really angry? List them. Do you believe this list would remain constant over a period of time; in other words, will you still be angry about these things months or years from now? Explain.

NINE-TENTHS OF THE WORLD'S ANIMAL POPULATION... IS NONHUMAN.

In the course of my reading I had come across a case where, many years ago, some hunters on our Great Plains organized a buffalo hunt for the entertainment of an English earl—that, and to provide some fresh meat for his larder. They had charming sport. They killed seventy-two of those great animals; and ate part of one of them and left the seventy-one to rot. In order to determine the difference between an anaconda and an earl—if any—I caused seven young calves to be turned into the anaconda's cage. The grateful reptile immediately rushed one of them and swallowed it, then lay back satisfied. It showed no further interest in the calves, and no disposition to harm them. I tried this experiment with other anacondas; always with the same result. The fact stood proven that the difference between an earl and an anaconda is that the earl is cruel and the anaconda isn't; and that the earl wantonly destroys what he has no use for, but the anaconda doesn't. It also seemed to suggest that the earl was descended from the anaconda, and had lost a good deal in the transition.

Mark Twain
LETTERS FROM THE EARTH

A journal is a private place. You write it, and you read it. Don't lie to yourself. Write yourself the truth, or as close as you can get to it.

The seven-year-old today has had a heavy dose of adult experiences and global imagery via TV. He enters grade school as an adult.

Marshall McLuhan
CULTURE IS OUR BUSINESS

There are 60 million homes in the United States and over 95 percent of them are equipped with a television set. (More than 25 percent have two or more sets.) In the average home the television is turned on some five hours forty-five minutes a day. The average male viewer, between his second and sixty-fifth year, will watch television for over 3000 entire days—roughly nine full years of his life. During the average weekday winter evening nearly half of the American people are to be found silently seated with fixed gaze upon a phosphorescent screen.

Americans receive decidedly more of their education from television than from elementary and high schools. By the time the average child enters kindergarten he has already spent more hours learning about his world from television than the hours he would spend in a college classroom earning a B.A. degree.

The academicians, research scientists and critics have been telling us for years of television's impact upon the attitudes and behavior of those who watch it. They cite very persuasive statistics to indicate that television's influence has affected, in one way or another, virtually every phenomenon in our present-day society.

Nicholas Johnson
HOW TO TALK BACK TO YOUR TELEVISION SET

My father has a face with very pronounced features. His domed forehead merges into a bald top, and his brow is crossed by deep ridges. He has a high and fleshy nose, and tiny, deep-set eyes which give an impression of sternness. This impression is further heightened by the thin and tightly closed lips, strong jaws, and a substantial chin. But this appearance is deceptive, for my father, although never given to gushy displays of emotion, is one of the gentlest and most affectionate men I have ever met.

Chris Noble
JOURNAL

Not all your entries need be in words. Try sketching some. Add captions if you wish.

Get the people you know into your journal. One interesting way is to list everything you can think of about a person. The first few things will come easily; this is the superficial view, just the surface of the person. Keep going. Make the list longer and longer until the person stands alone, unmistakably himself, to the full extent that you know him.

You might try this using yourself as the subject. It's much harder to be honest when writing about yourself.

Paul Bunyan was of tremendous size and strength, the strongest man that ever swung an ax. . . . He had curly black hair which his loving wife used to comb for him every morning with a great crosscut saw, after first parting it nicely with a broadax, and a big black beard that was as long as it was wide and as wide as it was long. He was rather proud of this beard, and took great care of it. Several times every day he would pull up a young pine tree by the roots and use its stiff branches in combing and brushing it smooth.

Wallace Wadsworth

Portrait of a Machine

What nudity is beautiful as this
Obedient monster purring at its toil;
Those naked iron muscles dripping oil
And the sure-fingered rods that never miss.
This long and shining flank of metal is
Magic that greasy labor cannot spoil;
While this vast engine that could rend the soil
Conceals its fury with a gentle hiss.

It does not vent its loathing, it does not turn
Upon its makers with destroying hate.
It bears a deeper malice; lives to earn
Its master's bread and laughs to see this great
Lord of the earth, who rules but cannot learn,
Become the slave of what his slaves create.

Louis Untermeyer

Select the largest object that you can see and describe its features. Are there any aspects of this object that cannot be seen from where you are? What do you think is hidden from your point of view?

Writing allows you tremendous freedom to consider alternatives, to try things out on paper. Think of an object. Try to list as many of its functions as you can. (To what uses could a pail be put?) Then list all the objects that could serve as functional substitutes for it. (What besides a pail could be used to carry water?)

Try to live a day without touching an electrical device.

9

During these last decades the interest in professional fasting has markedly diminished. It used to pay very well to stage such great performances under one's own management, but today that is quite impossible. We live in a different world now. At one time the whole town took a lively interest in the hunger artist; from day to day of his fast the excitement mounted; everybody wanted to see him at least once a day; there were people who bought season tickets for the last few days and sat from morning till night in front of his small barred cage; even in the nighttime there were visiting hours, when the whole effect was heightened by torch flares; on fine days the cage was set out in the open air, and then it was the children's special treat to see the hunger artist; for their elders he was often just a joke that happened to be in fashion, but the children stood open-mouthed, holding each other's hands for greater security, marveling at him as he sat there pallid in black tights, with his ribs sticking out so prominently, not even on a seat but down among straw on the ground, sometimes giving a courteous nod, answering questions with a constrained smile, or perhaps stretching an arm through the bars so that one might feel how thin it was, and then again withdrawing deep into himself, paying no attention to anyone or anything, not even to the all-important striking of the clock that was the only piece of furniture in his cage, but merely staring into vacancy with half-shut eyes, now and then taking a sip from a tiny glass of water to moisten his lips.

Franz Kafka
A HUNGER ARTIST

Ann Moore, aged 48, now living at Tutbury, in Staffordshire, has swallowed no kind of food whatever, either solid or fluid, for the last two years and a half. Her appetite began to decline about seven years ago, in consequence of a weak digestion, and in March 1807 the passage to her stomach became completely closed, so as not to admit of her swallowing even a drop of water; from the pit of her stomach downward she is a mere skeleton, notwithstanding which her countenance is perfectly cheerful, and has the appearance of good health. . . . She never sleeps, but amuses herself by reading all night, and receiving the visits of vast numbers who daily flock to her humble roof. Her memory is amazingly retentive and she feels no inconvenience but from the approach of persons who have been drinking spirits, which affects her much.

LONDON CHRONICLE (1809)

Happily our geography text, which contains maps of all the principal land-masses of the world, is large enough to conceal my clandestine journal-keeping, accomplished in an ordinary black composition book. Every day I must wait until Geography to put down such thoughts as I may have had during the morning about my situation and my fellows. I have tried writing at other times and it does not work. Either the teacher is walking up and down the aisles (during this period, luckily, she sticks close to the map rack in the front of the room) or Bobby Vanderbilt, who sits behind me, is punching me in the kidneys and wanting to know what I am doing. Vanderbilt, I have found out from certain desultory conversations on the playground, is hung up on sports cars, a veteran consumer of *Road and Track.* This explains the continual roaring sounds which seem to emanate from his desk; he is reproducing a record album called *Sounds of Sebring.*

Donald Barthelme

What are the sounds that fill your day? Tomorrow, try to keep track of them, and write them into your journal. What ones are pleasant? What ones annoying? Try to describe the different voices you hear during the day. Which sounds are, like music, interesting for themselves rather than for what they mean?

Go somewhere and listen. List several sounds. Repeat, using the senses of taste, smell, and touch in order.

Spanish was off-limits in school anyway, and teachers and relatives taught me early that my mother tongue would be of no help in making good grades and becoming a success. Yet Spanish was the language I used in playing and arguing with friends. Spanish was the language I spoke with my abuelita, my dear grandmother, as I ate atole on those cold mornings when I used to wake at dawn to her clattering dishes in the tiny kitchen; or when I would cringe in mock horror at old folk tales she would tell me late at night.

Armando B. Rendon
CHICANO MANIFESTO

Part of the power of language comes from its ability to express things that do not exist in the world: things that once existed but no longer exist, things that don't exist yet, even things that could never exist. Write about something important to you that no longer exists, something important that doesn't exist yet, and something important that could not exist.

Steam Shovel

The dinosaurs are not all dead.
I saw one raise its iron head
To watch me walking down the road
Beyond our house today.
Its jaws were dripping with a load
Of earth and grass that it had cropped.
It must have heard me where I stopped,
Snorted white steam my way,
And stretched its long neck out to see,
And chewed, and grinned quite amiably.

Charles Malam

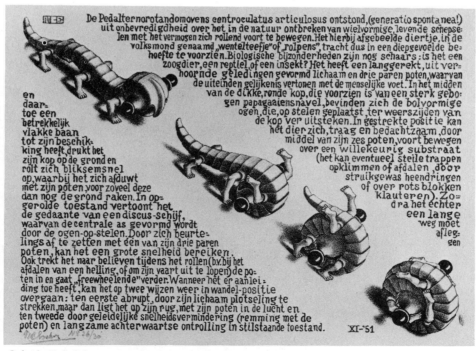

Curl-up by M. C. Escher, courtesy of Escher Foundation, Haags Gemeentemuseum, The Hague.

What geometric figures do you first perceive here? Why? Does one square seem to be in front of the other? Can you make the other seem to be in front?

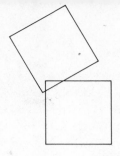

ephemeris n. (L from Gk *ephemeris* diary, calendar) . . . 3. (Obs.) a) an almanac, calendar; b) a diary; journal.

Try to explain something that puzzled you. What effect does writing about it have on your understanding of it?

You're probably wondering why I'm here . . . well, so am I . . . so am I.

Frank Zappa

March 31, 1966

1,000,000,000,000,000,000,000,000.00000000	miles to edge of known universe
100,000,000,000,000,000,000.00000000	miles to edge of galaxy (Milky Way)
3,573,000,000.00000000	miles to edge of solar system (Pluto)
205.00000000	miles to Washington, D. C.
2.85000000	miles to Times Square, New York City
.38600000	miles to Union Square subway stop
.11820000	miles to corner of 14th Street and First Avenue
.00367000	miles to front door of Apartment 1D, 153 First Avenue
.00021600	miles to typewriter paper page
.00000700	miles to lens of glasses
.00000098	miles to cornea from retinal wall

Dan Graham

He turned to the flyleaf of the geography and read what he had
written there: himself, his name and where he was.

Stephen Dedalus
Class of Elements
Clongowes Wood College
Sallins
County Kildare
Ireland
Europe
The World
The Universe

James Joyce
A PORTRAIT OF THE ARTIST AS A YOUNG MAN

Who am I? I am a human being that hates the public and likes to live with a companion somewhere alone, isolated from everyone else.

Where am I? Totally in wonder, always in wonder, like why does man live, why does the sun burn, why are there stars, good questions, any answers?

Why am I alive? Good question, I wish I could really find the answer, then I could help mankind.

When do I die? When the time of all has gone, when time has stopped, when everything dies is when I die, for eternity.

Michael Breen
JOURNAL

Look at yourself in a mirror for as long as you can take it. Write about what you see.

Interview yourself. Begin with something specific that you've done today or are planning to do. Then go on from there, asking questions that seem to follow from your answers. Good interviewers often try to start

with something small and very specific and then keep asking questions that are broader and more general. A successful interview could last for the life of the person being interviewed, if the interviewer wanted to keep asking questions. You needn't go that far, although in a sense that's what you'll be doing if you keep a journal all your life.

"All my life I pretended with my folks, it was the thing in the street that was real. I was certainly just pretending with the nuns and priests, . . . I was the ugliest, skinniest little misfit in the group. . . . My family knew very little of my real life. In effect, I lived two lives, the one with my mama and sisters, and the thing on the street. . . ."

George Jackson
SOLEDAD BROTHER: THE PRISON LETTERS OF GEORGE JACKSON

One of the first things I think young people, especially nowadays, should learn is how to see for yourself and listen for yourself and think for yourself. Then you can come to an intelligent decision for yourself. If you form the habit of going by what you hear others say about someone, or going by what others think about someone, instead of searching that thing out for yourself and seeing for yourself, you will be walking west when you think you're going east, and you will be walking east when you think you're going west. This generation, especially of our people, has a burden, more so than any other time in history. The most important thing we can learn to do today is think for ourselves.

It's good to keep wide-open ears and listen to what everybody else has to say, but when you come to make a decision, you have to weigh all of what you've heard on its own, and place it where it belongs, and come to a decision for yourself; you'll never regret it. But if you form the habit of taking what someone else says about a thing without checking it out for yourself, you'll find that other people will have you hating your friends and loving your enemies. This is one of the things that our people are beginning to learn today—that it is very important to think out a situation for yourself. If you don't do it, you'll always be maneuvered into a situation where you are never fighting your actual enemies, where you will find yourself fighting your own self.

Malcolm X
MALCOLM X SPEAKS

15

List ten things that you have done that you'd like to do again. Do you think they'd be different the second time you did them? How? Why?

The Old Man's Comforts and How He Gained Them

You are old, Father William, the young man cried,
  The few locks which are left you are grey;
You are hale, Father William, a hearty old man,
  Now tell me the reason, I pray.

In the days of my youth, Father William replied,
  I remember'd that youth would fly fast,
And abused not my health and my vigour at first,
  That I never might need them at last.

You are old, Father William, the young man cried,
  And pleasures with youth pass away;
And yet you lament not the days that are gone,
  Now tell me the reason, I pray.

In the days of my youth, Father William replied,
  I remember'd that youth could not last;
I thought of the future, whatever I did,
  That I never might grieve for the past.

Robert Southey

Father William

"You are old, Father William," the young man said,
"And your hair has become very white;
And yet you incessantly stand on your head—
Do you think, at your age, it is right?"

"In my youth," Father William replied to his son,
"I feared it might injure the brain;
But now that I'm perfectly sure I have none,
Why, I do it again and again."

"You are old," said the youth, "as I mentioned before,
And grown most uncommonly fat;
Yet you turned a back-somersault in at the door—
Pray what is the reason of that?"

"In my youth," said the sage, as he shook his gray locks,
"I kept all my limbs very supple
By the use of this ointment—one shilling the box—
Allow me to sell you a couple."

Lewis Carroll

What was the most expensive thing you ever bought? How did you get the money for it? Was it worth it?

A close friend of mine, an accountant, told me of an experience he had recently when he audited the books of a corporation. It became apparent that the office manager was dipping into the petty cash to the extent of about $2,000 a year. He reported this fact to the president. The president responded, "How much are we paying him?" "Ten thousand a year," replied the accountant. "Then keep quiet about it," said the president. "He's worth at least $15,000."

Lawrence R. Zeitlin

17

The largest amount of cash ever found and returned to its owners was $240,000 in unmarked $10 and $20 bills found in a street in Los Angeles, by Douglas William Johnston in March, 1961. He received many letters, of which 25 percent suggested that he was insane.

GUINNESS BOOK OF WORLD RECORDS

At the highway woods I took one good look to make sure no cruisers were up or down the road and I dove right in the woods. It was a lot of dry thickets I had to crash through, I didn't want to bother finding the Boy Scout trail. I aimed straight for the golden sands of the riverbottom I could see up ahead. Over the thickets ran the highway bridge, no one could see me unless they stopped and got out to stare down. Like a criminal I crashed through bright brittle thickets and came out sweating and stomped ankle deep in streams and then when I found a nice opening in a kind of bamboo grove I hesitated to light a fire till dusk when no one'd see my small smoke, and made sure to keep it low embers. I spread my poncho and sleeping bag out on some dry rackety grove-bottom leaves and bamboo splitjoints. Yellow aspens filled the afternoon air with gold smoke and made my eyes quiver. It was a nice spot except for the roar of trucks on the river bridge. My head cold and sinus were bad and I stood on my head five minutes. I laughed, "What would people think if they saw me?" But it wasn't funny, I felt rather sad, in fact real sad, like the night before in that horrible fog wire-fence country in industrial L.A., when in fact I'd cried a little. After all a homeless man has reason to cry, everything in the world is pointed against him.

Jack Kerouac

Waiting

I am waiting.
On benches, at the corners
of earth's waitingrooms,
by trees whose sap rises, rises
to escape in gray leaves and lose
itself in the last air.
Waiting
for who comes at last,
late, lost, the forever
longed-for, walking
not my road but crossing
the corner where I wait.

Denise Levertov

chronicle n., v. (ME *cronicle* from AF from L *chronica* from Gk *chronika* annals, chronology) n. 1. a record of events arranged in the order of time; a history. v.t. 2. to record; to register.

A journal is an ideal place to tell secrets or record rumors and your reactions to them.

Deceit

The fox when he sees a flock of magpies or jackdaws or birds of this kind, instantly throws himself on the ground with mouth open in such a way as to seem dead: the birds think to peck at his tongue and he bites off their heads.

Leonardo Da Vinci
THE NOTEBOOKS OF LEONARDO DA VINCI

SEND ONE COPY TO:
REGISTRAR OF MOTOR VEHICLES
100 NASHUA STREET
BOSTON, MASS. 02114

ONE COPY TO:
POLICE DEPARTMENT in whose juris-
diction the accident occurred.

MUST TYPE OR PRINT

COMMONWEALTH OF MASSACHUSETTS
OPERATOR'S REPORT
OF MOTOR VEHICLE ACCIDENT

REGISTRY USE ONLY

2-7

8-10

19
Was this Accident investigated by an Officer?
If Yes, Check One Box Below

1 ☐ Registry		4 ☐ State Police
2 ☐ MDC		5 ☐ Local Police
3 ☐ Other		

11-15 Date of Accident — Mo. Day Yr.

16 Day of the Week

S	M	T	W	T	F	S
1	2	3	4	5	6	7

A.M. ☐ X   P.M. ☐ Y

17 Hour

18 Have you completed a Mass. driver education course   YES ☐ X   NO ☐ Y

VEHICLE 1

Name of Operator Making Report

20 Number of Vehicles Involved.

21-26 Date of Birth — MO. DAY YR.

27 Sex   1 ☐ M   2 ☐ F

Street Address   City/Town   State

28-29 License Number and State

Owners Name and Address (if same, write "same")

Registration Number & State

Name of Insurance Company only may be written here   Year   Make   Type   Approximate Cost to Repair $

Describe Damage to Vehicle:

Parked Car   YES ☐   NO ☐

VEHICLE 2

Name of Operator

30-35 Date of Birth — MO. DAY YR.

36 Sex   1 ☐ M   2 ☐ F

Street Address   City/Town   State

37-38 License Number and State

Owners Name and Address (if same, write "same")

Registration Number & State

Name of Insurance Company only may be written here   Year   Make   Type   Approximate Cost to Repair $

Describe Damage to Vehicle:

Parked Car   YES ☐   NO ☐

OTHER

Describe Other Property Damage

Approximate Cost to Repair $

Name of Property Owner   Address

WITNESSES

Other Witnesses or Persons Present	Address	Phone
		Bus.
		Res.

39 Number Injured.   To what hospital was injured taken?

INJURED 1

Name of Injured   Street   City/Town   State

40-1 Age

42 Sex   1 ☐ M.   2 ☐ F.

43 Check if wearing Seat Belt   1 ☐

44 Check if Wearing Helmet   1 ☐

45 Severity — Mark First One That Applies

Killed	as bleeding wound, or distorted member; or had to be carried from scene	Visible signs of injury,	Other visible injury, as bruises, abrasions, swelling, limping, etc.	No visible injury but complaints of pain or momentary unconsciousness
	1 ☐	2 ☐	3 ☐	4 ☐

46 Person Injured

1	Operator } in vehicle	
2	Passenger } No. ___	6 ☐ Pedestrian
3	Passenger in train, bus, etc.	7 ☐ Bicyclist
4	Operator } On Motorcycle	8 ☐ Other
5	Passenger }	

INJURED 2

Name of Injured   Street   City/Town   State

47-8 Age

49 Sex   1 ☐ M.   2 ☐ F.

50 Check if wearing Seat Belt   1 ☐

51 Check if Wearing Helmet   1 ☐

52 Severity — Mark First One That Applies

Killed	Visible signs of injury, as bleeding wound, or distorted member; or had to be carried from scene	Other visible injury, as bruises, abrasions, swelling, limping, etc.	No visible injury but complaints of pain or momentary unconsciousness
	1 ☐	2 ☐	3 ☐	4 ☐

53 Person Injured

1	Operator } in vehicle	
2	Passenger } No. ___	6 ☐ Pedestrian
3	Passenger in train, bus, etc.	7 ☐ Bicyclist
4	Operator } On Motorcycle	8 ☐ Other
5	Passenger }	

INJURED 3

Name of Injured   Street   City Town   State

40-1 Age

42 Sex   1 ☐ M.   2 ☐ F.

43 Check if wearing Seat Belt   1 ☐

44 Check if Wearing Helmet   1 ☐

45 Severity — Mark First One That Applies

Killed	Visible signs of injury, as bleeding wound, or distorted member; or had to be carried from scene	Other visible injury, as bruises, abrasions, swelling, limping, etc.	No visible injury but complaints of pain or momentary unconsciousness
	1 ☐	2 ☐	3 ☐	4 ☐

46 Person Injured

1	Operator } in vehicle	
2	Passenger } No. ___	6 ☐ Pedestrian
3	Passenger in train, bus, etc.	7 ☐ Bicyclist
4	Operator } On Motorcycle	S ☐ Other
5	Passenger }	

In politics, one only escapes deception by knavery or irony, and never proceeds from an evil to a good, but from one bad condition to another. One can be happy when the last is less bad than the one that preceded it; this is what is called progress.

Henri Frédéric Amiel
PRIVATE JOURNAL

Great ideals are the glory of man alone. No other creature can have them. Only man can get a vision and an inspiration that will lift him above the level of himself and send him forth against all opposition or any discouragement to do and to dare and to accomplish wonderful and great things for the world and for humanity. . . . There can be no conquest to the man who dwells in the narrow and small environment of a groveling life, and there can be no vision to the man the horizon of whose vision is limited by the bounds of self. But the great things of the world, the great accomplishments of the world, have been achieved by men who had high ideals and who have received great visions. The path is not easy, the climbing is rugged and hard, but the glory at the end is worth while . . . .

LECTURE NOTES OF MATTHEW A. HENSON

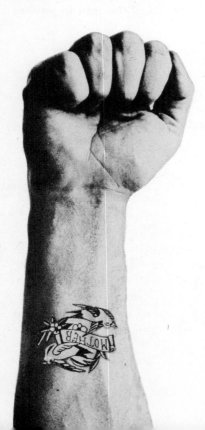

21

The female borrowing wasp makes a most considerate mother. She takes great care to see that her children will have a supply of fresh food when they hatch from their eggs after she has died. She attacks, say, a spider; but she does not kill it. Instead, she paralyzes it by inserting her stinger carefully into the nerve center of her victim. She continues until she has quite a collection, which she leaves beside her eggs. When the eggs hatch and the larva swarm out, they find close at hand a source of live, fresh food, unable to run or to fight off the hungry youngsters.

Lily's useless information—She told me today about an old woman who was supposed to have the parakeet with the world's biggest vocabulary (for a bird). It knew some scientific terms and slang words and the names of all the world leaders and the words to popular songs. The strange part—when the parakeet died, its last statement was "I love mama."

Suzy Steinberg
JOURNAL

For an entry or two, shift the focus of your journal from yourself to someone you know and like. Devote as much care and thought to writing about that person as you would to yourself.

Madness

As the wild bull hates the colour red the hunters drape in red the trunk of a tree, and the bull charges it furiously and gets his horns fixed in it, and then the huntsmen kill him.

Leonardo Da Vinci
THE NOTEBOOKS OF LEONARDO DA VINCI

Year 2000, April 43

This is a day of great jubilation. Spain has a king. They've found him. *I* am the king. I discovered it today. It all came to me in a flash. It's incredible to me now that I could have imagined that I was a civil-service clerk. How could such a crazy idea ever have entered my head? Thank God no one thought of slapping me into a lunatic asylum. Now I see everything clearly, as clearly as if it lay in the palm of my hand. But what was happening to me before? Then things loomed at me out of a fog. Now, I believe that all troubles stem from the misconception that human brains are located in the head. They are not: human brains are blown in by the winds from somewhere around the Caspian Sea.

Marva was the first to whom I revealed my identity. When she heard that she was facing the King of Spain, she flung up her hands in awe. She almost died of terror. The silly woman had never seen a King of Spain before. However, I tried to calm her and, speaking graciously, did my best to assure her of my royal favor. I was not going to hold against her all the times she had failed to shine my boots properly. The masses are so ignorant. One can't talk to them on lofty subjects. Probably she was so frightened because she thought that all kings of Spain are like Philip II. But I carefully pointed out that I wasn't like Philip II at all. I didn't go to the office. The hell with it. No, my friends, you won't entice me there now; never again shall I copy your dreadful documents.

Nikolai Gogol
THE DIARY OF A MADMAN

'DIVA' LIVES AS STAR AT BAVARIAN HOTEL—TILL SHE HAS TO SING
SPECIAL TO *THE NEW YORK TIMES*

BONN, May 27—She billed herself as Maria della Metastasia, the grand diva from Milan's La Scala Opera, and lived the life of a star for a month in a Bavarian resort hotel. But when the manager finally persuaded her to sing for her supper, she hit so many false notes that he called the police.

The police of the town of Wunsiedel disclosed today that Maria della Metastasia was really Maria Bittner, 43 years old, of Kassel, a one-time choral singer who had been jailed before for fraud.

Miss Bittner is in jail again, on charges of having swindled a total of $1,675 out of the Crown Prince of Bavaria Hotel and several cosmetic and dress shops in Wunsiedel.

THE NEW YORK TIMES

When Joseph Palmer moved to Fitchburg, Massachusetts, in the 1830's, the townspeople denounced him as "un-American," "a human monster," and similar epithets—all because he wore a long beard.

Palmer was hooted on the street, sometimes pelted with stones and clods of earth, and his son's boyhood was made miserable by schoolmates who taunted him because of his father's beard.

Despite his persecution—which included a year's imprisonment in the county jail for defending himself against four husky attackers bent on shaving his beard—Palmer dared to be different—and kept his beard.

Before he died at the age of eighty-four in 1875 most of the men who had condemned him were wearing beards themselves.

Bill Severn

24

An observant person can learn a lot about someone from a quick inspection of his room. Try it with your room, with the room of a friend, or with the living room of someone you visit. What could a stranger learn about you by spending a half hour in your room without disturbing anything? What can you learn about other people in the same manner? Why does this work?

The room in which I found myself was very large and lofty. The windows were long, narrow, and pointed, and at so vast a distance from the black oaken floor as to be altogether inaccessible from within. Feeble gleams of encrimsoned light made their way through the trellised panes, and served to render sufficiently distinct the more prominent objects around; the eye, however, struggled in vain to reach the remoter angles of the chamber, or the recesses of the vaulted and fretted ceiling. Dark draperies hung upon the walls. The general furniture was profuse, comfortless, antique, and tattered. Many books and musical instruments lay scattered about, but failed to give any vitality to the scene. I felt that I breathed an atmosphere of sorrow. An air of stern, deep, and irredeemable gloom hung over and pervaded all.

Edgar Allen Poe
THE FALL OF THE HOUSE OF USHER

My Living Room

It ain't big but big enough for me and my family—my wife Rosie setting over there reading recipes in the Birmingham *News* and my two girls Ellen Jean and Martha Kay watching the TV. I am setting here holding *Life* magazine in my lap. I get *Life,* the *News,* and *Christian Living.* I read a lots, the newspaper everyday from cover to cover. I don't just look at the pictures in *Life.* I read what's under them and the stories. I consider myself a smart man and I ain't bragging. A man can learn a lots from just watching the TV, if he knows what to watch for and if he listens close. I do. There ain't many that can say that and be truthful. Maybe nobody else in this whole town.

Tom McAfee
THIS IS MY LIVING ROOM

Saw two men in the Mexican restaurant eating hot chili and tostados and drinking beer—many beers. I guess the combination of the beers and the chili brought tears to their eyes, because this was their conversation:

FIRST MAN: Hey, what're you crying about?

SECOND MAN: Ah, I'm just sad to see old Tony go.

Then a pause.

SECOND MAN: Hey, what're *you* crying about?

FIRST MAN: I'm just sorry you didn' go with 'im.

My way of joking is to tell the truth; it's the funniest joke in the world.

George Bernard Shaw

It was twenty degrees below zero in North Dakota, and a man working on the platform near the top of an oil derrick began to ride down on a crane, against the wishes of his foreman who stood shouting at him to "stay up there."

When the man reached the ground, the foreman asked, "What did you come down for?"

"Ah'm going to get my jacket," the man drawled.

"Well, where did you leave it?" the foreman asked.

"In Florida," was the nonchalant answer.

Herbert V. Prochnow

26

A man, sitting with a friend at a theater, said to him between the acts: "Do look across at that woman in the box next the stage. Did you ever see such a fright?"

The man looked, and said, with evident embarrassment, "That's my sister."

"No, no," said the first speaker, trying to save the situation. "I don't mean the one you're looking at. I mean the awful-looking guy at the other side of the box."

"That," said his friend, "is my wife."

Stephen Leacock

Have you ever seen a film showing a flower opening up? The technique used is known as time-lapse photography; individual pictures are taken at certain intervals and when shown consecutively condense what may have actually taken days or weeks into a few minutes of film. Adapt this technique for some of your journal entries: at selected intervals observe and write about something in the process of change. Does this technique work as well for writing as it does for film-making? Why or why not?

Have I said it before? I am learning to see. Yes, I am beginning. It still goes badly. But I intend to make the most of my time.

To think, for instance, that I have never been aware before how many faces there are. There are quantities of human beings, but there are many more faces, for each person has several. There are people who wear the same face for years; naturally it wears out, it gets dirty, it splits

27

at the folds, it stretches, like gloves one has worn on a journey. These are
thrifty, simple people; they do not change their face, they never even
have it cleaned. It is good enough, they say, and who can prove to them
the contrary? The question of course arises, since they have several faces,
what do they do with the others? They store them up. Their children will
wear them. But sometimes, too, it happens that their dogs go out with
them on. And why not? A face is a face.

Rainer Maria Rilke
THE NOTEBOOKS OF MALTE LAURIDS BRIGGE

**Your friends won't look the same forever. They're growing older
every day. How do they look and act now?**

What one uses in war.
(1) What everyone knows about.
(2) The despair of those who don't want to fight.
(3) The pride of those whom nothing compelled to leave but who left
in order to avoid being alone.
(4) The hunger of the men who enlist because they have lost their job.
(5) Many noble feelings like:
(a) solidarity in suffering.
(b) contempt that wants to remain silent.
(c) the absence of hatred.
It is all put to a despicable use and it all leads to death.

Albert Camus
NOTEBOOKS, 1935-1942

Primitive man found diversion from the tedium of life by taking
from his more thrifty neighbour the things he was too idle to provide for
himself. When he learnt the team spirit he banded himself with kindred
souls to satisfy his needs at less risk to himself. His neighbour in
self-defence sought assistance from his friends, and thus War, elementary
and unsophisticated it is true, came to be born.

War afforded primitive man his chief escape from the rigours of
agriculture and family life. When not occupied by fighting, he spent his
leisure hours listening to minstrels singing the praises of heroes and
'battles long ago.'

Brigadier P. Young and Lieutenant Colonel J. P. Lawford
CHARGE! OR HOW TO PLAY WAR GAMES

28

Nonviolence does not seek to defeat or humiliate the opponent, but to win his friendship and understanding. The nonviolent resister not only refuses to shoot his opponent but he also refuses to hate him. To strike back in the same way as his opponent would do nothing but increase the existence of hate in the universe. Along the way of life, someone must have sense enough and morality enough to cut off the chain of hate.

In the final analysis all life is interrelated. All humanity is involved in a single process, and all men are brothers. To the degree that I harm my brother, no matter what he is doing to me, to that extent I am harming myself. Why is this? Because men are brothers. If you harm me, you harm yourself.

Martin Luther King, Jr.,
MARTIN LUTHER KING EXPLAINS "NONVIOLENT RESISTANCE"

How salty are the oceans? Which is the saltiest?

Salinity in the open ocean normally ranges from 3.3 to 3.7%. Oceanographers express salinity in parts per thousand; the symbol for parts per thousand is o/oo. The average is about 35 o/oo. The saltiest ocean is the Atlantic, with 37.5 o/oo in the northern subtropical region. The Pacific is less salty than the Atlantic because it is affected less by dry winds and resulting high evaporation rates. In the deeper waters of the Pacific, the salinity ranges from 34.6 o/oo to 34.7 o/oo. The Arctic and Antarctic waters are the least salty.

Some areas in the world have abnormally high salinities; for example, the Red Sea and the Persian Gulf have salinities exceeding 42 o/oo. The "hot, salty hole" in the Red Sea has salinities exceeding 270 o/oo (close to saturation) at depths below 2,000 meters.

Very low salinities occur where large quantities of fresh water are supplied by rivers or melting ice. Salinity in the Baltic is 2 o/oo to 7 o/oo and in the Black Sea about 18 o/oo.

U.S. Naval Oceanographic Office

Make a list of questions you'd like answered.

What is the volume of the world's oceans?

Estimates vary from 317 to 330 million cubic miles; the most reliable sources place the volume at approximately 328 million cubic miles. Ocean waters comprise about 85 percent of the total water on the earth's surface.

The volume of all land above sea level is only one-eighteenth of the volume of the ocean. If the solid earth were perfectly smooth (level) and round, the ocean would cover it to a depth of 12,000 feet.

U.S. Naval Oceanographic Office

What, for you, is the difference between a "good" day and a "bad" day?

FRIDAY 11 FEBRUARY. Nothing worth putting into my journal occurred this day. It passed away unnoticed, like the whole life of many a person.

James Boswell
LONDON JOURNAL (1763)
[adapted slightly]

HI THERE!

Look, love

                    ******
                    (00)
                            springs

from out the

                    ******
                    (oo)
                    ()
                            surface of a pedestrian

fact, a new

                    ******
                    (oo)
                    ()
                    (____)
                            day.

Robert Creeley

The Day Everything Went Wrong

Well the first thing that went wrong was at breakfast. I spilled milk all over the table. Then while I was cleaning it up the bus went down by. So my father brought me to school. I was in such a hurry I jumped out of the car and got my dress caught on the door handle and ripped it. Then I was running down the stairs and fell. (Brother was I ever embarrassed.) On my way to lunch I bumped into Mr. Fairfield. In gym class I got onto the balance beam and fell off and hurt my ankle. I failed my math test, and when I told my parents they bawled me out. Then after doing the dishes I went upstairs to read; I turned the light on and got a shock because I hadn't dried my hands good enough.

Kathy Hescock
JOURNAL

Tuesday

Yesterday I helped my little brother catch ants. He had been given an ant farm—minus ants—for his birthday on Thursday and ever since then had been pestering me to catch some ants for him. We had ants in the kitchen—my mother was always complaining about them and putting these little circular ant traps all over the place—but he needed a couple of dozen ants for his farm so I decided we should try to find a nest outdoors. That way we could easily scoop up what we needed and be done with it.

It didn't work out as smoothly as I had hoped. We found the ants quickly enough—under a small rock—but they didn't take kindly to being picked up. They climbed up and over the walls of the bowl as fast as I put them in; one even bit my finger. It took a long time to collect our two dozen ants, but we finally finished and, after I nearly dropped the bowl carrying it back into the house, managed to get them all into the ant farm.

Charles Norton
JOURNAL

The night was dark and cold. The wind was wild. One of us in the group around the fire—I don't remember who—said that it reminded him of the night his brother disappeared. We asked him to tell the story.

Reluctantly, he began.

"The night was dark and cold. The wind was wild. One of us in the group around the fire—I don't remember who—said that it reminded him of the night his brother disappeared. We asked him to tell the story.

"Reluctantly, he began.

"'The night was dark and cold. . . .

Can you make the top triangle look like the bottom one by moving only 3 circles?

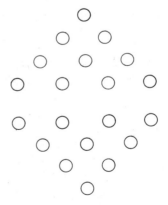

Two men have been working all day, trying to solve a difficult problem. At the end of the day one man has solved it, and one has not.

32

"I've solved it," says the short one.

"I haven't," says the tall one.

If at least one of the men is lying, which one has actually solved the problem?

Does it seem as if the same old things happen day after day? Don't let yourself believe that. If you think about some of those "same" things, probe them, speculate about them, and write them down, you'll find they aren't the "same" at all. The reason is that you're not the same day after day.

Life can seem dull and repetitious if you assume it is dull and repetitious. Don't. Keep looking for more and keep writing it down.

The Second Coming

Turning and turning in the widening gyre
The falcon cannot hear the falconer;
Things fall apart; the centre cannot hold;
Mere anarchy is loosed upon the world,
The blood-dimmed tide is loosed, and everywhere
The ceremony of innocence is drowned;
The best lack all conviction, while the worst
Are full of passionate intensity.

Surely some revelation is at hand;
Surely the Second Coming is at hand.
The Second Coming! Hardly are those words out
When a vast image out of Spiritus Mundi
Troubles my sight: somewhere in sands of the desert
A shape with lion body and the head of a man,
A gaze blank and pitiless as the sun,
Is moving its slow thighs, while all about it
Reel shadows of the indignant desert birds.
The darkness drops again; but now I know
That twenty centuries of stony sleep
Were vexed to nightmare by a rocking cradle,
And what rough beast, its hour come round at last,
Slouches towards Bethlehem to be born?

William Butler Yeats

Brahma, the first living creature within the universe, created several sons for the propagation of various kinds of species. The most powerful among his sons is Bhrigu, who is the greatest sage. Of all transcendental vibrations, Om (the Omkara) is the representation of Krishna. Of all sacrifices, the chanting of Hare Krishna, Hare Krishna, Krishna Krishna, Hare Hare / Hare Rama, Hare Rama, Rama Rama, Hare Hare, is the purest representation of Krishna.

A. C. Bhaktivedanta Swami
THE BHAGAVAD GITA AS IT IS

List ten foods that you like, ten you dislike, and ten you have never tried. Refer back to this list after a few months have passed. Have there been any shifts in your preferences?

About half the beef eaten in the United States is eaten in the form of hamburger—some 11.3 billion pounds of it a year, or a yearly average of about 55 pounds of hamburger for every man, woman and child in the country. If what CU recently found in one city is at all typical of ground meat sold nationwide, the heavy consumption of hamburger looks like a great, but often unwarranted, act of faith. A shockingly large percentage of the hamburger we purchased was well on the way to putrefaction. A good number of our samples contained more fat than unadulterated hamburger would normally; some samples contained more fat than the law allows. And our results hint that at least some ground meat labeled as chuck or round may be something else.

CONSUMER REPORTS, AUGUST 1971

© King Features Syndicate, Inc., 1971.

34

April 16, 1767

5 in the afternoon - I have just been eating my Chicking, sitting over my repast upon it, with Tears - a bitter Sause - Eliza! but I could eat it with no other - when Molly spread the Table Cloath, my heart fainted within me - one solitary plate - one knife - one fork - one Glass! - O Eliza! twas painfully distressing, - I gave a thousand pensive penetrating Looks at the Arm chair thou so often graced on these quiet, sentimental Repasts - & sighed & laid down my knife & fork, - & took out my handkerchief, clap'd it across my face & wept like a child.

Laurence Sterne
THE JOURNAL TO ELIZA AND VARIOUS LETTERS

Your stomach is a hollow sac surrounded by muscles. When you put food in your stomach, these muscles contract and break up the food, forcing it into the rest of your digestive tract. About three hours after you have eaten, all the food has passed out of your stomach, but the muscles continue to contract. This contraction of the empty stomach causes it to growl and produces hunger pangs. These pangs, which are most intense in healthy young people and which will persist with increasing severity until you have gone three or four days without food (after that time they will gradually weaken), can be stilled by the ingestion of a small amount of food. Food is not the only thing, however, that can cause your hunger pangs to cease. You can allay them temporarily by swallowing hard, tightening your belt, or even eating some non-nutritive and indigestible substance. If we ate only to satisfy our hunger, we would follow a pattern different than most of us are accustomed to: we would eat smaller quantities at more frequent intervals. Usually our hunger is allayed well before we get through our meal—and it is certainly not hunger that explains why we attack our dessert with such relish.

diary n. (L *diarium* daily allowance, hence record of this, from *dies,* day) 1. a daily written record, especially of the writer's own experiences, thoughts, etc. 2. a book for keeping a record of personal notes and memoranda.

Suppose that you are an imaginary someone, someone who doesn't know you at all but has stumbled upon your journal. Reread your journal with the eyes of this stranger. What is your opinion of the writer, your assessment of his mind, his heart, his life?

35

Lord Bute, when young, possessed a very handsome person, of which advantage he was not insensible; and he used to pass many hours every day, as his enemies asserted, occupied in contemplating the symmetry of his own legs.

Sir Nathaniel Wraxall
HISTORICAL MEMOIRS, 1836

To see the world as others see it—very difficult. To see ourselves as others see us—even more difficult. But try. After you've spent some time with someone, write about the experience in your journal, not as you experienced it, but as you think he may have. What do you suppose he thought of you? What did he find admirable, repellent, or memorable? What did he learn from you?

It is well, when one is judging a friend, to remember that he is judging you with the same Godlike impartiality.

Arnold Bennett

. . . Went to Tony's house to eat dinner. In the living room all the furniture looks like something cut out on a jigsaw, like pieces of a picture puzzle. Found out from Tony that it was made just that way. His father found the plans in a magazine and liked them so much that he bought a jigsaw, which Tony says he's still paying for, and made all these chairs and tables.

After dinner Tony's father shows me how his easy chair works. It has levers and springs that adjust it to any position you want. Something went wrong in the making of it, though, and the spring tensions are all wrong. To get it to recline (which you'd try to do when you were tired) takes all the strength you can manage. On the other hand, when you press the lever to return to a sitting position, the back shoots up so fast that you're thrown out of the chair and the back legs actually lift off the floor. Nonetheless, Tony's father is very proud of it.

Ed Conley
WHAT GOES ON HERE? (A JOURNAL)

When was the last time your own possibilities gave you goosepimples?

Write a kind of annual report on the state of yourself. Compared to what you were a year ago, what are you now? What do you hope to be a year from now? What do you expect to be? Do you expect to make "progress" in your life? If so, what goals do you hope to progress toward? If you don't expect progress, what kind of change do you look for? Hope for?

I have before me two photographs. One is, I regret, instantly recognizable: a bald man, sitting before a pastry board propped on a table, and writing. He does little else besides sit and write. His fattish face is supported by a valance of chins; the head is held together by glasses that slip down a bridgeless nose that spreads its nostrils over a moustache. He is trying to find some connection with the figure in another picture taken fifty years ago. He knows that the young fellow sitting on the table of a photographer's in Paris, a thin youth of twenty with thick fairish hair, exclaiming eyebrows, loosely grinning mouth, and the eyes raised to the ceiling with a look of passing schoolboy saintliness, is himself. The young one is shy, careless, very pleased with himself, putting on some impromptu act; the older one is perplexed. The two, if they could meet in the flesh, would be stupified, and the older one would certainly be embarrassed.

V. S. Pritchett
"STARTING TO WRITE: PARIS, 1921," FROM MIDNIGHT OIL

Childhood is *forgetful* and *forgiving;* the first is an evil, the second is a good. Children require again and again to be reminded of their duty and interest; and there are few things more difficult, than to make lasting impressions on their minds; trifling things too often make a more lasting impression than important ones; and both resolutions and lessons are often equally forgotten. In children, however, bad impressions often share the fate of good ones, and that frailty which cannot retain the good, provides for the escape of the bad. These then are the obvious characters of youth and of childhood. It is the morning of life when every thing is yet to be learned; the preparations for effort, when every thing is yet to be done. It is a stage between torpidity and activity, the prelude to the scenes of life, and the birth-day of the future man. Ah, happy day! the sweetest and the fairest of life! Unruffled by perplexing cares, unembittered by a guilty conscience, and unbeclouded by dark forbodings or prevailing fears! The reign of innocence and the heaven of earth!

Thomas Martin (1818)

How swiftly life passes here below! The first quarter of it is gone before we know how to use it; the last quarter finds us incapable of enjoying life. At first we do not know how to live; and when we know how to live it is too late. In the interval between these two useless extremes we waste three-fourths of our time sleeping, working, sorrowing, enduring restraint and every kind of suffering. Life is short, not so much because of the short time it lasts, but because we are allowed scarcely any time to enjoy it. In vain is there a long interval between the hour of death and that of birth; life is still too short, if this interval is not well spent.

Jean-Jacques Rousseau

Come, fill the Cup, and in the Fire of Spring
The Winter Garment of Repentance fling:
The Bird of Time has but a little way
To fly—and Lo! the Bird is on the Wing.
Omar Khayyam

38

memorandum n. (pl. *memoranda*) (L *memorandus* to be remembered)
1. a) a short note written to help one remember something or remind
one to do something. b) a record of events or observations, especially
one for future use . . .

**What, above all else, do you wish you could do, experience, or think
about tomorrow?**

Today is the first day of the rest of your life.

Into the Future

Standing here just short of the corner
I grope with fingertips
against the rasping surface of brick.
If it had handholds I would hang on.
One move could ruin everything.
They would find my blood running down the wall.

In times like these
one never retraces steps. Forward
is the only direction. Beyond this corner
the wind gusts cold, coughing wave—
whirls of dust along Michigan Avenue.
If I let go and turn the corner
what will come at me from my blind side?
A newspaper clutches at my leg and forces me on.

Peter Davison

What are you looking forward to?

One good result of World War II was that it cleaned up the
junkyards completely. Every piece of metal in this country, as well as in
others, was sent off "to win the war." Housewives flattened every tin can
after it was opened, putting it aside for the special collections.
Unnecessary metal objects of all shapes and sizes joined the war effort. At
least for a while, the metal was being used.

Suzanne Hilton
HOW DO THEY GET RID OF IT?

**Everyone accumulates junk, old and often odd things that collect in
a drawer or closet, attic, or basement. They seem useless now, but we
can't quite bring ourselves to get rid of them. Go through some of your
accumulated junk and write the story behind something you find there.**

"Tut, tut, child!" said the Duchess. "Everything's got a moral, if only you can find it." And she squeezed herself up closer to Alice's side as she spoke.

Alice did not much like her keeping so close to her: first because the Duchess was *very* ugly; and secondly, because she was exactly the right height to rest her chin upon Alice's shoulder, and it was an uncomfortably sharp chin. However, she did not like to be rude, so she bore it as well as she could. "The game seems to be going on rather better now," she said.

"'Tis so," said the Duchess, "and the moral of it is—'Oh, 'tis love, 'tis love, that makes the world go round!'"

"Somebody said," whispered Alice, "that it's done by everybody minding their own business!"

"Ah, well! It means much the same thing," said the Duchess, digging her sharp little chin into Alice's shoulder as she added, "and the moral of *that* is—'Take care of the sense, and the sounds will take care of themselves.'"

"How fond she is of finding morals in things!" Alice thought to herself.

"I dare say you're wondering why I don't put my arm round your waist," the Duchess said after a pause: "the reason is, that I'm doubtful about the temper of your flamingo. Shall I try the experiment?"

"He might bite," Alice cautiously replied, not feeling at all anxious to have the experiment tried.

"Very true," said the Duchess: "flamingoes and mustard both bite. And the moral of that is—'Birds of a feather flock together.'"

"Only mustard isn't a bird," Alice remarked.

"Right, as usual," said the Duchess: "what a clear way you have of putting things!"

"It's a mineral, I *think*," said Alice.

"Of course it is," said the Duchess, who seemed ready to agree to everything that Alice said; "there's a large mustard-mine near here. And the moral of that is—'The more there is of mine, the less there is of yours.'"

Lewis Carroll
ALICE IN WONDERLAND

I knew a gentleman who was so good a manager of his time, that he would not even lose that small portion of it which the calls of nature obliged him to pass in the necessary-house; but gradually went through all the Latin Poets in those moments. He bought, for example, a common edition of Horace, of which he tore off gradually a couple of pages, carried them with him to that necessary place, read them first, and then sent them down as a sacrifice to Cloacina; this was so much time fairly gained; and I recommend to you to follow his example. It is better than only doing what you cannot help doing at those moments; and it will make any book which you shall read in that manner very present in your mind.

Lord Chesterfield
LETTERS WRITTEN BY LORD CHESTERFIELD TO HIS SON

Right now, based on your experience, what practical information about life, living, and growing up could you give to a younger person?

There are three things that a gentleman, in following the Way, places above all the rest: from every attitude, every gesture that he employs he must remove all trace of violence or arrogance; every look that he composes in his face must betoken good faith; from every word that he utters, from every intonation, he must remove all trace of coarseness or impropriety.

Confucius
ANALECTS

analects n. pl. (L *analecta* from Gk *analekta* to collect, from *ana* up + *le-gein,* to gather), collected literary excerpts or fragments of writing; as, the Analects of Confucius.

How early are your earliest memories? Can you remember what you were like ten years ago?

42

WHEN I WAS ABOUT FIVE OR SIX, I DECIDED THAT ONE OF LIFE'S
GREATEST INJUSTICES WAS NOT BEING ABLE TO CHOOSE YOUR OWN PARENTS.

Curt Graves
JOURNAL

Truth

Although partridges steal each other's eggs, nevertheless, the
children born from these eggs always return to their true mother.

Leonardo Da Vinci
THE NOTEBOOKS OF LEONARDO DA VINCI

September 2d.—"When I grow up," quoth Julian, in illustration of
the might to which he means to attain,—"when I grow up, I shall be
two men."
September 3d.—Foliage of maples begins to change. Julian, after
picking up a handful of autumnal maple-leaves the other day,—"Look,
papa, here's a bunch of fire!"

Nathaniel Hawthorne
AMERICAN NOTEBOOKS (1850)

July 31. I spent much of the day today watching the moon-walk on
TV. I thought I was going to write pages about the importance of it, the
cost of it, the tension, and my reactions, but instead there is one little
thing about the time I spent there that strikes me. My little brother and
two of his friends came in to watch for a while, but quickly got bored.
One of them had just learned to play solitaire. He showed the others how
to play, and then they all sat there playing solitaire and arguing about
what they could or couldn't do with the cards, while this great triumph of
technology was on the screen. The new card game meant much more to
them.

Henry Beebe
JOURNAL

Tuesday, April 6

Sandy and Phyllis came over last night and told the weirdest story. A couple of days ago they had a fight, and while they were still mad at each other and not talking, Sandy went out on the balcony to cool off. He was just about ready to go in and make up when he tripped on a can of suntan lotion and almost fell off the balcony. He was hanging by his hands from the tenth floor, and he's sure the fall would have killed him. When he went inside he was shaking and laughing hysterically. What he found so funny was the idea that if he had fallen and been killed, Phyllis would've thought she drove him to suicide. That's funny?

(name withheld)
JOURNAL

Suicides

| | 1960 | | 1965 | | 1966 | | 1967 | |
	M	F	M	F	M	F	M	F
Poisoning	2,631	1,699	3,179	2,816	2,970	2,618	2,949	2,746
Hanging and strangulation	2,576	790	2,453	744	2,231	632	2,112	666
Firearms and explosives	7,879	1,138	8,457	1,441	8,780	1,627	8,766	1,784
Other	1,453	875	1,401	1,016	1,435	988	1,360	942
TOTAL	14,539	4,502	15,490	6,017	15,416	5,865	15,187	6,138

ENCYCLOPEDIC ALMANAC

Resume

Razors pain you;
Rivers are damp;
Acids stain you;
And drugs cause cramp.
Guns aren't lawful;
Nooses give;
Gas smells awful:
You might as well live.

Dorothy Parker

Record the gradual changes that occur in your immediate environment as the seasons change. Watch for changes in the air, sunlight, plants, people's attitudes, plans and concerns, clothing, and the rhythm and tempo of life.

. . . Up till now, this Journal is still a strange, hybrid being, a letter-rack, a memorandum book, a minute of proceedings, an investigator, a confidant, a witness, . . . it is a bore in any case. And so it is far from amusing to reread. But writing it has been useful to me, and so it has its excuse.

Henri Frédéric Amiel
PRIVATE JOURNAL
[adapted slightly]

Instead of writing about today, or after you've written about today, let your memory take over. Reach back to something from your past. Don't bother with my-greatest-most-exciting-moment. Go after something real— a memory so vivid that you can smell some of it, almost touch it. It might begin with anything, even something small like a kitchen sound, a child- hood game, or the memory of a hot day.

```
yesterdayyesterday      rdayyest      yestermorrow            row      tomor          rowto
yesterdayyesterday    sterdayyesterd  yestermorrowtom          rrowt    morr           rrow
yesterdayyesterday    esterdayyesterda yestermorrowtomo        orrowto  orro     orro
       dayyes       yester      terday yester      wtomor    morrowtom   rrowtomor
       dayyes       yeste       erday  yester        tomor  omorr wtomo   owtomo
       dayyes       yester      terday yester    wtomor  tomor     tomor   owtomo
       dayyes     esterdayyesterda     yestermorrowtomo  wtomorrowtomorr   owtomo
       dayyes     sterdayyesterd       yestermorrowtom  owtom        morro owtomo
       dayyes       rdayyest           yestermorrow     rowto      orrow owtomo
```

Carl Neublatt

The whole interior of the place was hot as the living hell. Most of us would have on just a pair of overalls or some old hip pants; we didn't wear shirts. The water in the drinking pipes at the time was hot enough to take a bath in, and the men were always thirsty for a drink of cool water.

Some of the men would get 20 and 40 gallon barrels and put 100 pounds of ice in each of them, filling them with water; then they would charge everybody 15 cents a week. There were many of us, with sweat running off our half-naked bodies like rain, who didn't seem to know how to stop drinking, once we started. We'd just stand there gulping down that cold, refreshing water, and the next thing we'd know there'd be a fellow or two knocked out with cramps. There was always a stretcher in the box beside the wall, and when a man fell out, a couple of guys ran and got the stretcher, put him on it and hurried him on to the so-called doctor's office. From there they would rush him to the company's hospital. Sometimes, we would get the news the next day that Jim or Big Red or Shorty or Slim was dead.

The company's responsibility—besides furnishing the stretchers—was $500 for the family if the worker died; if he lived and was out two weeks or more, they paid him $9 a week up to nine weeks.

Hosea Hudson
A BLACK WORKER IN THE DEEP SOUTH

What do you like about the area where you live? What do you dislike about it?

Before and after Levittown.

48

Train yourself to see. When you look at a specific car, do you see it simply as a car or as, for example, a dirty, pale blue 1965 Dodge Dart? List 25 visual specifics about a place or object.

The automobile is an extension of the house. Young people used to court in the parlor, then on the front porch, then in the automobile—the porch-on-wheels. Today, the porch-on-wheels may be observed at the local drive-in movie "house." Movies are better than ever.

R. Buckminster Fuller
I SEEM TO BE A VERB

record v.t. (ME *recorden* from L *recordari* to call to mind; remember, from *re* again + *cor* heart, mind) 1. to set down, as in writing; preserve an account of . . .

I mentioned that Lord Monboddo told me he awaked every morning at four, and then for his health got up and walked in his room naked, with the window open, which he called taking an air bath; after which he went to bed again, and slept two hours more.

James Boswell

The happiest part of a man's life is what he passes lying awake in bed in the morning

Samuel Johnson

49

commonplace n. (literal translation of the Latin *locus communis,* Greek *koinos topos* general topic) 1. originally, a passage marked for reference, or a collection of such passages in a book called a *commonplace book . . .*

What is worth writing about in your journal? Anything that you think is worth thinking, talking, or writing about.

> *the cockroaches are not*
> *the only insects*
> *that are demanding more*
> *consideration*
> *i met a flea*
> *last evening who*
> *told me that he had come*
> *into contact with*
> *a great deal of unrest*
> *lately and a mosquito remarked*
> *to me only this*
> *morning there is darned*
> *little justice in this world the*
> *way the human beings*
> *run it seldom do i*
> *meet a person who will hold*
> *still long*
> *enough for me to get a meal*
>   *archy*
>
>   *Don Marquis*
> THE LIVES AND TIMES OF ARCHY & MEHITABEL

Spiders may not be among your favorite creatures, but they are a helpful ally to man in controlling insects. With a little understanding about how a spider, for example the orb weaver, catches and kills insects—a spider is not, as is often assumed, an insect himself—you may begin to appreciate how the spider helps to control the insect population. His first step is to spin a web. He does this by drawing thin strands of silk out of jets located near the back of his body. These strands, which are stronger than steel wire of the same diameter, are stretched and woven into a web. The spider then perches on an out-of-the-way part of the web, his sensitive claws ready to pick up the vibration produced when an insect, such as a fly, lands in the web. As soon as the insect hits the web, the spider scurries quickly toward him—the sticky substance on the strands makes a temporary prisoner of the insect—and paralyzes him with a single bite. The spider then wraps the immobilized insect in a film of silk. If he is hungry he may eat his prey at once, if not the insect will be there for him when he is ready. A single spider may catch and destroy a hundred or more insects a year, and when we consider that an acre of meadowland may contain 50,000 or more spiders, we can appreciate the spider's role in the natural control of insects.

Perhaps you've seen "open letters" in newspapers. In an open letter a person writes to an individual or to an organization presenting views on something the person or group has done. The writer then publishes the letter so that other people will know his or her views. Try putting some of your views into your journal in the form of open letters.

51

WE NOW BRING YOU AN UNACCUSTOMED SOUND.

THE CLASH OF OPINIONS.

In response to polls of high-school students taken in 1970,

48% of boys said they would enlist in an all-volunteer army;

38% of girls said they would enlist;

39% of all students felt the United Nations "is important to keep";

33% had no opinion about the Vietnam war;

74% favored extending the vote to 18-year-olds;

31% felt that no "dress code" should be enforced in public schools;

90% felt they should be involved in curriculum planning and setting rules of conduct;

59% said marijuana was available at their schools;

47% said that for help with a personal problem they would turn first to a friend.

figures from SCHOOL AND SOCIETY, FEBRUARY 1971

I just don't like guns. I don't want anybody to have them. People who talk about this or that group being better armed than another are talking as if they were playing some sort of game where you move gun pieces around to best advantage. They couldn't realize that in real life you don't draw a card that says "dead," you feel bullets tearing into you and breaking your bones and leaving holes out of which all your blood runs as you lie in the gutter dying. I don't want that to happen to any person, including persons who for good or bad or no reasons are cops. There must be better ways to fight guns than with guns, and if there aren't we ought to think up some. If we get guns we're just like them and have no right or reason to fight them and everybody would be better off without us.

James Simon Kunen
THE STRAWBERRY STATEMENT

Record the opinions of at least three other persons on a particular issue. Add your own opinion. Do you all agree? Disagree? Why?

Past lake and rockery
Laughing when he shook his paper
Hunchbacked in mockery
Through the loud zoo of the willow groves
Dodging the park keeper
With his stick that picked up leaves.

The hunchback in the park
A solitary mister
Propped between trees and water
From the opening of the garden lock
That lets the trees and water enter
Until the Sunday sombre bell at dark

And the old dog sleeper
Alone between nurses and swans
While the boys among willows
Made the tigers jump out of their eyes
To roar on the rockery stones
And the groves were blue with sailors

Eating bread from a newspaper
Drinking water from the chained cup
That the children filled with gravel
In the fountain basin where I sailed my ship
Slept at night in a dog kennel
But nobody chained him up.

Made all day until bell time
A woman figure without fault
Straight as a young elm
Straight and tall from his crooked bones
That she might stand in the night
After the locks and chains

Like the park birds he came early
Like the water he sat down
And Mister they called Hey mister
The truant boys from the town
Running when he had heard them clearly
On out of sound

All night in the unmade park
After the railings and shrubberies
The birds the grass the trees the lake
And the wild boys innocent as strawberries
Had followed the hunchback
To his kennel in the dark.

                                        Dylan Thomas

Find a drawing or photograph that conveys the feeling of loneliness. Describe the feeling in your own words.

There may be something so important to you, something that makes such a strong impression, that you'd like to try building a poem around it. Go ahead. No one but you will judge your success or failure.

> Woe to him that is alone when he falleth; for he hath not another to help him up.
>
> Ecclesiastes, IV, 10

If this is "primitive" . . .

Anthropologist Dr. Ralph Solecki led an expedition to Iraq that uncovered the skeletons of nine Neanderthals—six men, two women, and a child—that they named Shanidar I-IX.

Shanidar I was forty years old when he died. Solecki explained that this was very old for a Neanderthal, equal to the age of eighty today. All his life Shanidar I was a cripple: his right arm, shoulder, and collar bone were deformed from birth; the arm was amputated when he was a child; his skull showed that when he was young he suffered a skull fracture that blinded his left eye; he had had another fracture on the top of his skull, a serious one, at some other time in his life.

Neanderthal life was incredibly difficult; harder than modern man can imagine. And yet Shanidar I, who was of no use to others and couldn't even take care of himself, lived to the equivalent of eighty. How? Evidence convinced Dr. Solecki that he was entirely supported by the people he lived with, who respected him enough that they built a monument, a pile of stones, over his grave, and buried him with flowers.

. . . what's "civilized"?

Cambridge, Mass. (UPI)—A statement from a "women's revolutionary group" claiming to have bombed Harvard University's Center for International Affairs has been rejected by police officers.

"This was a very sophisticated bomb," a Cambridge police officer said Thursday, describing the device which destroyed a library in the center. "We feel that women wouldn't be capable of making such a bomb."

GLOUCESTER DAILY TIMES, OCTOBER 16, 1971

One interesting aspect of a journal can be its use as a collecting box. It can house, in words, almost any kind of collection. For example:

witty quotations
odd place names
original insults
epigrams and other pithy bits of wisdom
drawings, sketches
graffiti
memorable descriptions

Anishinabemowin is a language of verbal forms and word images. The spoken feeling of the language is a moving image of tribal woodland life: nibi—water, mang—loon, makwa—bear, amik—beaver, kingfishers at dusk, the owls at night, and maple syrup in the snow.

The language is euphonious: Anishinabe nagamon—songs of the people, pipigwan—flute, manomin—wild rice, gimiwan—rain, sibi—river, memengwa—butterfly, nibawin—sleeping, sisibakwat—maple sugar, ishkote—fire, papakine—grasshopper, wawatessi—firefly.

And the words are descriptive: missanwi—snow falling from the branches, kijiga—maple sap is running fast from the trees, onabani gisiss—the month of the moon on the crust of the snow, sagashka—grass begins to grow, papakine magad ishkote—crackling fire.

Gerald Vizenor
ANISHINABE NAGAMON (SONGS OF THE PEOPLE)

What kind of life would you like to lead? What would a typical day of that life be like?

Design a place to live, and design a life for yourself there. Daydream about it. Record your daydreams in your journal. It might be a simple dwelling for you alone and a life lived entirely away from people. It might be a city house for a fast-paced city life. Your home might even be in an entirely new city, built where none had been before or in a utopian society as large as a nation.

The Lake Isle of Innisfree

I will arise and go now, and go to Innisfree,
And a small cabin build there, of clay and wattles made:
Nine bean-rows will I have there, a hive for the honeybee,
And live alone in the bee-loud glade.

And I shall have some peace there, for peace comes dropping slow,
Dropping from the veils of the morning to where the cricket sings;
There midnight's all a glimmer, and noon a purple glow,
And evening full of the linnet's wings.

I will arise and go now, for always night and day
I hear lake water lapping with low sounds by the shore;
While I stand on the roadway, or on the pavements grey,
I hear it in the deep heart's core.

William Butler Yeats

Write a blues song about your life.

Houston (AP)—The University of Texas board of regents took steps Friday to stop its spiraling enrollment on the Austin campus by initiating a one-year pilot program.

However, Frank C. Erwin, regents board chairman, said he disapproves of any enrollment policy that limits admission to "A" students.

"I'll never vote for a permanent plan to limit enrollment on the basis of grades only," he said. "If we adopted such a plan, then in three or four years we would have nothing but "A" students at Austin. And we would be in the same position as Berkeley University of California where disturbances have occurred."

THE EL PASO TIMES, OCTOBER 24, 1970

Make a list of the things you would like changed about your school.

Springtime Study Hall Blues

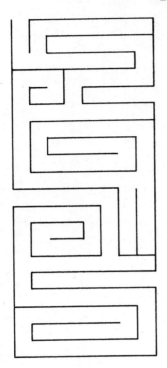

It isn't easy,
this sitting inside when it's springtime.
You get restless
and feel like jumping up
and running out the door
into the world
—without a corridor pass.
The Whisperers shrill
back and forth
across the rows of desks.
You can't sleep.
You listen to the noises of monotony:
pencils scratching
fingers drumming
pages idly turning
pens tapping. . . .
You watch the clouds move
or stare at the ripples of heat
rising from the radiators
past the open windows.
Your eyes feel heavy
and your leadweighted feet ache
to be barefoot and pounding against the
packed sands
of a hot windy beach.
Outside, a truck roars past
and everything vibrates for a brief
instant.
Floors, desks, students—
everything comes wavering to life
and nods back into death.
You glance at the clock on the front wall
and sigh.

S. Danny Riemer

In 1749, the Duke of Montague, Lord Portman, and some other noblemen were talking about the gullibility of the people, and the Duke offered this wager. Let a man advertise the most impossible thing in the world, and he would find fools enough in London to fill a playhouse and pay handsomely for the privilege of being there. "Surely," said the Earl of Chesterfield, "if a man should say that he would jump into a quart bottle, nobody would believe that." The bet was made and the following advertisement was inserted in the papers of January, 1749.

At the New Theatre in the Hay market, on Monday next, the 12th instant, is to be seen a Person who performs the several most surprising things following, viz.—1st. He takes a common walking Cane from any of the Spectators, and thereon plays the music of every Instrument now in use, and likewise sings to surprising perfection.—2dly. He presents you with a common Wine Bottle, which any of the spectators may first examine; this Bottle is placed on a Table in the middle of the Stage, and he (without any equivocation) goes into it, in the sight of all the Spectators, and sings in it: during his stay in the bottle, any Person may handle it, and see plainly that it does not exceed a common Tavern Bottle.—Those on the Stage, or in the Boxes, may come in masked habits (if agreeable to them); and the Performer, if desired, will inform them who they are.—Stage, 7s. 6d. Boxes, 5s. Pit, 3s. Gallery, 2s. Tickets to be had at the Theatre:—To begin at half an hour after six o'clock. The performance continues about two hours and a half.

Note.—If any Gentlemen or Ladies (after the above Performance) either single or in company, in or out of mask, is desirous of seeing a representation of any deceased Person, such as Husband or Wife, Sister or Brother, or any intimate Friend of either sex, upon making a gratuity to the Performer, shall be gratified by seeing and conversing with them for some minutes, as if alive; likewise, if desired, he will tell you your most secret thoughts in your past Life, and give you a full view of persons who have injured you, whether dead or alive. For those Gentlemen and Ladies who are desirous of seeing this last part, there is a private Room provided.

These performances have been seen by most of the crowned Heads of Asia, Africa, and Europe, and never appeared public any where but once; but will wait on any at their Houses, and perform as above, for five Pounds each time. A proper guard is appointed to prevent disorder.

On the appointed day the theatre was overflowing with people. When the performer failed to make an appearance, the audience started to riot. The theatre was practically demolished. They gutted the building and carried everything burnable out into the street for a giant bonfire.

Dick Sutphen
THE MAD OLD ADS

Try summing up what has happened to you, what you've thought and felt, what you've written since you began keeping this journal.

Make a list of words that rhyme with your name. For example, if your name is Jane, your list might include the following: brain, cellophane, chain, crane, drain, Duquesne, entertain, gain, grain, hurricane, reign, rein, Spain, sprain, train, urbane, vain, vane, and vein.

Try to write a limerick about yourself using some of the words you have listed.

"I—I hardly know, sir, just at present—at least I know who I was when I got up this morning, but I think I must have been changed several times since then."

Make a catalog listing all your relatives. You might then incorporate some of this information into a family tree.

Robin and Richard

Robin and Richard,
Two young city men,
Lay in bed
Till the clock struck ten;
Then up starts Robin
And looks at the sky,
Oh, brother Richard,
The sun's very high.
No matter, says Richard,
What time it may be,
There are no jobs
For you or for me.

Eve Merriam

"I quit school when I were sixteen."

The animals were recognizably animals, and that was about all you could say for them—but it was something you could not have said for any of the other paintings there. The students had learned all the new ways to paint something (an old way, to them, was a way not to paint something) but they had not had anything to paint. The paintings were

paintings of nothing at all. It did not seem possible to you that so many
things could have happened to a piece of canvas in vain. You looked at
a painting and thought, "It's an imitation Arshile Gorky; it's casein and
aluminum paint on canvasboard, has been scratched all over with a razor
blade, and then was glazed—or scumbled, perhaps—with several
transparent oil washes." And when you had said this there was no more
for you to say. If you had given a Benton student a pencil and a piece of
paper, and asked her to draw something, she would have looked at you
in helpless astonishment: it would have been plain to her that you knew
nothing about art. By the time a Benton artist got through exploiting the
possibilities of her medium, it was too dark to do anything else that day;
and most of the students never learned that there was anything else to
do.

Randall Jarrell
PICTURES FROM AN INSTITUTION

Two Guys Get Out Of a Car

Two guys get out of a car.
They stand beside it. They
don't know what else to do.

Richard Brautigan

"To a large
extent,
we have
created in
our system
of higher
education
a machine
for the
destruction
of our
society." M. Stanton Evans
From the CBS News Opinion Series. SPECTRUM

The Difference in Conduct of Young Men Toward Ladies.

Corner Loungers Commenting on Passers-By.

Genial, Pleasant and Gentlemanly.

THE corner-idler, chewing tobacco, or smoking, lounging on boxes or against posts, talking foolishly and profanely, and leering at ladies as they pass, is an object of scorn and hatred, foreshadowing the depraved and dissolute man he will become.

IN HIS association with women, the young man who has a proper estimation of himself will always be polite, friendly and agreeable to the young ladies, manifesting respect and gentleness toward those who are older. Early politeness paves the way to successful manhood.

"Now, if I write 'n-e-w' on the blackboard, tell me what does it spell?"

"New."

"Now, I'll put 'k' in front of it, and what does it spell?"

"Canoe."

Herbert V. Prochnow

The ocean ahead has assumed a dazzling texture, brighter, whiter—than an ice field! It turns dazzling white in sunlight as it slides in beneath my wing. I feel that I'm entering the Arctic. Even those patches of snow on the bleak hillsides of Cape Breton Island did not prepare me for this change. I knew, of course, that my route lay north of the ship lanes, and that ships keep south because of the floating ice; but I wasn't ready to be transported so quickly to a frozen sea.

Great white cakes are jammed together, with ridges of crushed ice pushed up around the edges, all caught and held motionless in a network of black water which shows through in cracks and patches as I pass. A quarter mile in from the field's edge, the sea smooths out, the waves disappear, and there's not a sign of movement among the blocks of ice. As far as I can see ahead, the ocean is glaring white. Despite the noise and vibration of the engine, I feel surrounded by the stillness of a Minnesota winter—the frozen silence of the north. I feel a trespasser in forbidden latitudes, in air where such a little plane and I have no authority to be.

Charles A. Lindbergh
THE SPIRIT OF ST. LOUIS

All day long we have been gliding through the Gulf of Suez between two fantastically picturesque and desolate lands: Sinai, a great massif of granite and slashed red sandstone, and the Egyptian coast, at first regular and tabular and then bristling with all sorts of extraordinary peaks, all equally sharp and bare. Above them, dreamlike colours, strangely soft for a climate of such extremes. To the east, the sea seemed dark blue. Its line on the horizon was as sharp as a knife blade. And then, above this dark band, without a break, the pale pink of the mountains rose up into a misty green sky. At sunset, it was the western coast which drew to itself all the beauty of the evening. As the sun disappeared in a little flutter of burning clouds, so the mountains of Egypt, until then covered in mist, began to pass through every possible shade of violet, from the very deepest to the most transparent mauve. Last to be seen was a whole line of sharp points, like the teeth of a saw, silhouetted in the golden sky.

Pierre Teilhard de Chardin
LETTERS FROM A TRAVELLER

64

September 9, 1970—The whole world is raining, at least as far as I can see from my window. It's as if we were all sitting in some enormous pot and today someone put the lid on. Sad and ugly. Everything is gray—gray from my window to the next building, gray from the sidewalk on up. I see nothing but gray. In fact, I seem to taste gray, and when I stick my arms out in this, I touch gray. Things are dying, or dead, all the life, all the colors, all the happiness. The tops of the buildings seem to have dissolved into the sky. What do birds do on a day like this? Here I am with electric lights, a TV to distract me, books, magazines, food in the refrigerator—the day is ugly and depressing, so I turn away from it—but the birds, what can they do? Wait. Wait for the world to change away from gray. Hope that it does. After all, isn't that what all of us do?

We wait. Wait for what? Who knows? For things to get better, I guess. We hope. Hope for what? Whatever it is each of us wants. Money? Beauty? Something unusual to happen? What idiots.

Bob Auciello
JOURNAL

I am writing in order to look as if I were writing, in this small barbershop from which the summer heat is shut out; the physical charm of this hour; the barber's silent bustle; a fly occasionally annoys me.

André Gide
THE JOURNALS OF ANDRÉ GIDE

Some days, when you write in your journal, write with no plan at all in mind. Just sit down and write as much as you can, as fast as you comfortably can, for as long as you can, in whatever way you want, about whatever comes to your mind. Just wander wherever your thoughts take you.

An interesting variation of this kind of journal writing is to write everything that comes to mind after you've put yourself into an environment that is likely to affect what you think about. Try it on a noisy street corner, on a park bench, in the bathtub, on a desert, in front of the TV, on a subway, on a mountaintop, . . .

310P PST NOV 26 68 LA243

L BHA106 PD BEVERLY HILLS CALIF 26

DEAREST DARLING STOP YOU'RE BREAKING MY HEART STOP I AM A PRISONER
FOR SADNESS IS A PIT STOP OUR LOVE WAS SHORT STOP BUT OH SO PURE
YOU'VE GOT TO UNDERSTAND IT'S YOU THAT I ADORE STOP I WOULD BE
HAPPY ANYWHERE WITH US STOP UP IN AN AIRPLANE OR EVEN IN A BUS STOP
IF YOU DON'T COME BACK STOP MY FUTURE'S HEXED STOP I'M NOT SURE
JUST WHAT WILL HAPPEN TO ME NEXT STOP LOVE

MASON

Mason Williams
THE MASON WILLIAMS READING MATTER

Why did I send Alice that note? I feel terrible now. I was really burned at the time—she had no business pulling that stuff with Rick. Maybe I should have told him off too. I don't know. I felt that she had done it deliberately to hurt me—but I can't think of any reason why she would want to. I've never seen her be cruel to anyone. And she's certainly liked by a lot of the kids—that ought to mean something.

I acted without thinking—I should have confronted her—given her a chance to explain—maybe she would have apologized and I could have forgiven her and we could still be friends. I sure wish I hadn't sent that note.

Connie Noyes
JOURNAL

66

Message to deep-sea diver: "Surface at once. Ship is sinking."

Marshall McLuhan
CULTURE IS OUR BUSINESS

Food is important (vital, in fact) to all of us. An individual's eating habits are highly personal. How important is food to you? What are your likes and dislikes? How do they seem to fit with the rest of your personality?

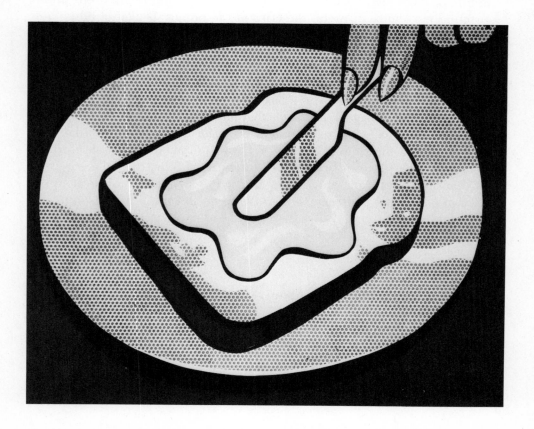

Vegetables are a real untapped gold mine of value for many of us. We need meat, too, but not nearly as much as most Americans eat. Perhaps we should arrange our meals as do people in many foreign countries—fill up on plant protein foods before tackling the meat course. We Americans tend to wade right into the roast beef before taking the edge off our appetites, and as a result, our arteries fill up with cholesterol faster than anyone else's.

Robert Rodale
ORGANIC GARDENING AND FARMING

A special class of beggars consists of those who beg after nine o'clock at night. You stand at your window, and suddenly see new faces, beggars you haven't seen all day. They walk out right into the middle of the street, begging for bread. Most of them are children. In the surrounding silence of night, the cries of the hungry beggar children are terribly insistent, and, however hard your heart, eventually you have to throw a piece of bread down to them—or else leave the house. These beggars are completely unconcerned about curfews, and you can hear their voices late at night, at eleven and even at twelve. They are afraid of nothing and of no one. There has been no case of the night patrol shooting at these beggars, although they move around the streets after curfew without passes. It's a common thing for beggar children like these to die on the sidewalk at night. I was told about one such horrible scene that took place in front of 24 Muranowska Street where a six-year-old beggar boy lay gasping all night, too weak to roll over to the piece of bread that had been thrown down to him from the balcony.

Emmanuel Ringelblum
NOTES FROM THE WARSAW GHETTO

What are the most repetitious, common, ordinary things that have occurred today?

Invent a monster and describe him.

Write a fantasy. You may use as a model one or more of the fairy tales that you heard as a child.

68

Once upon a time there were Three Bears, who lived together in a house of their own, in a wood. . . .

One day, after they had made the porridge for their breakfast, and poured it into their porridge-pots, they walked out into the wood while the porridge was cooling, that they might not burn their mouths, by beginning too soon to eat it. And while they were walking, a little old Woman came to the house. She could not have been a good, honest old Woman; for first she looked in at the window, and then she peeped in at the keyhole; and seeing nobody in the house, she lifted the latch. The door was not fastened, because the Bears were good Bears, who did nobody any harm, and never suspected that any body would harm them. So the little old Woman opened the door, and went in; and well pleased she was when she saw the porridge on the table. If she had been a good little old Woman, she would have waited till the Bears came home, and then, perhaps, they would have asked her to breakfast; for they were good Bears,—a little rough or so, as the manner of Bears is, but for all that very good-natured and hospitable. But she was an impudent, bad old Woman, and set about helping herself.

Robert Southey
THE DOCTOR

Naru stretched his six arms high over his head and inhaled the damp morning air through each of his twelve mouths. Continuing to flex his snaky limbs in the chilly atmosphere of the dimly lighted cell, he slowly filled the air sacs behind each of his mouths and then simultaneously shut them, letting the airy membranes which served as protective flaps close down over the tiny openings.

Variety enables us to distinguish between intervals such as short duration and long duration, or long duration and very long duration. Variety is a factor in boredom, while the degree of boredom experienced depends on how rapidly time passes.

We look for variety in occupations, careers, and hobbies. Our public "demands" a variety of material objects, food, clothing, and so forth. Consider for a moment the fact that few of us can say what we are going to have for lunch or dinner three days from now, let alone next year. Yet there are millions of people in the world who know exactly what they are going to have, if they are to have anything at all. They will eat the same thing they had today, yesterday, and the day before.

For us it is a matter of importance whether or not there is variety in life. Take the teen-age girl who complains to her mother that there weren't any boys at the dance, meaning that there weren't any new boys. Our demand for variety and for something new would seem to exceed that of almost any other culture in the world today. It is necessary to an economy like ours. Without constant innovation we could never keep our industrial plant expanding.

Edward T. Hall
THE SILENT LANGUAGE

For in and out, above, about, below,
'T is nothing but a Magic Shadow-show
Play'd in a Box whose Candle is the Sun,
Round which we Phantom Figures come and go.

Omar Khayyam

log n. (ME *logge,* akin to ON *lāg* felled tree) . . . 3. a daily record of a ship's speed and progress; logbook: in it are usually entered the ship's position and any notable events of the trip. . . .

Forget about trying to write about a "typical" day in your life. When you look back at such writing in the future, you'll find it empty and worthless, and not even "typical."
Write about *this* day.

April 22, 1851 . . . Journal neglected, journal wearisome; for it records only a few clumsy facts and few or no impressions; it preserves the matter and loses the spirit of the days that roll by. . . . A journal that does not keep up with life is not a journal at all, ... A witness who does not tell the whole truth is as much a false witness as one who perverts it, and more so than one who tells nothing. Therefore write every day . . . .

Henry Frédéric Amiel
PRIVATE JOURNAL

I had now and then mentioned my journal to him. I read him a little of it this evening. To be sure it is very carelessly wrote, which he freely took notice, and said it might become a habit to me to write in that manner, so that I would learn a more slatternly style. He advised me to take more pains upon it, and to render it useful by being a good method to practice writing: to turn periods and render myself ready at different kinds of expression. He is very right. I shall be more attentive for the future, and rather give a little neatly done than a good deal slovenly.

James Boswell
LONDON JOURNAL

Adopt some sort of time-saving device for writing your journal entries. This might be, for example, shorthand symbols or abbreviations.

A good photographer is rarely without his camera. This means that in order to have it with him when the right picture comes along, he will have to carry it with him all the time. A writer doesn't have to carry such heavy gear around; his equipment is much lighter and smaller—a pen or pencil and some paper.

Explain how some complicated piece of machinery (a vending machine, for example) might work. Compare your explanation with one that you can find in a reference book. *The Way Things Work: An Encyclopedia of Modern Technology* is one good source.

Use your journal to record any wild ideas you get for inventions, writ-ings, or whatever.

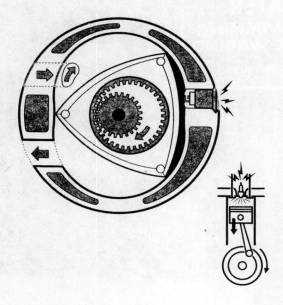

Ignition. As the rotor face moves down the comparatively flat side wall, the gas is ignited and expanded, providing the thrust to keep the rotor turning. At right, ignition propels the piston on its downward "power stroke." The Wankel should be cheaper for the car owner to maintain (with roughly 630 parts vs. 1,030 for a typical piston engine of the same horsepower) and could cost, by one estimate, from 15 to 35 per cent less to produce.

At work Mr. Slade has bought a new machine that cuts french fries. "This is gonna help us keep up with the McDonald's stand," he claims, and he is always showing the machine to friends of his who come into the diner. But what he hasn't noticed is that it used to take me an hour to cut all the french fries for the next day, and now it takes two hours, using the machine.

The old cutter was just a screen—just thin wires in a square pattern on a metal frame. All I had to do was put the screen over a peeled potato and push. Presto—french fries. Now I start by cleaning the machine ("Very important," says Slade), then I stand by the machine and drop the potatoes in one at a time—ONE AT A TIME—("Very important," says Slade). About every dozen potatoes, they start coming out more like pretzels than french fries. That's because the little leftover pieces on the edges that I used to throw away as I cut each potato build up in the chute where the cut french fries fall out. If you let it keep going (I tried) the already cut pieces get so jammed up that they stick back up into the cutters and get cut again—into little chunks. And if you let it go long enough, presto—mashed potatoes. I told Slade he should hire a very small man to stand inside with a very small broom.

John Maguire
JOURNAL

In order for the average person living in United States society today to continue to live the kind of life to which he has become accustomed, nearly 25 tons of material must be removed from the earth in one form or another. Twenty-five tons for each person each year.

It is not known exactly when man identified pollution as a problem. Not only was it beneath the dignity of ancient writers to discuss the matter; it wasn't an issue. Pollution was a part of life.

History does, however, record that the early Romans complained that a black soot in the air smudged their togas. And in merry old England there was once a law prohibiting the burning of a certain low grade of coal. Violation was punishable by death, and King Edward I (1272-1307 A.D.) is known to have enforced the penalty.

Gene Gregory
THE UNESCO COURIER

Average Solid Waste Collected
(Pounds per person per day)

Solid wastes	Urban	Rural	National
Household	1.26	0.72	1.14
Commercial	0.46	0.11	0.38
Combined	2.63	2.60	2.63
Industrial	0.65	0.37	0.59
Demolition, construction	0.23	0.02	0.18
Street and alley	0.11	0.03	0.09
Miscellaneous	0.38	0.08	0.31
TOTALS	5.72	3.93	5.32

data from HEW

THE WALLS BELONG TO THE PEOPLE

If you look at the inside of any building, public or private, you will notice a heck of a lot of blank space. You will see that the walls of our society's houses are just a big empty yeck! There is nothing on them to show any sign that there are any humans in the immediate vicinity. We have all of this great socio-political communications media going to waste because of a stupid property hang-up!

It's certainly a melancholy comment on this lousy society that a clean wall is more valued than a human expression, but it's the truth. At the beginning of a course in English Lit or Government what is the first thing the humans in the classroom are told? "DO NOT WRITE ON THE DESK TOPS! I REPEAT, DO NOT WRITE ON THE DESK TOPS!" At least 7 different people sit in a single desk in one day, most of whom are probably strangers to each other. Yet in the interest of Clean, Hygienic, Sterile, Blank desk tops we have to forego a chance to communicate with 7 strangers. I might have something to say to you but this damn desk top won't let me.

Moving out into the world the possibilities are even greater. How many people pass that blank concrete wall over there? I could not even guess, but I could write them all something except I might get busted for "defacing public property." If we can't write on our own wall where can we write? No—the public doesn't own the property, the property seems to own the public.

People of society, unite! Escape from those clean gray walls! Throw off your Magic Marker caps! The walls, sidewalks, bridges, desk tops, and phone booths belong to the people!

HOW OLD WILL YOU BE IN 1984?
(edited by Diane Divoky)

Do not write in this space

Because it is a private place, a journal is ideal for criticizing yourself. In what ways do you wish you were a different person? In what ways do you hope you'll change? You might try writing this as notes to your future self.

Occasionally one of your teachers may be asked to write a report about you. How would you write this report if you were he or she? Would your version agree with the teacher's?

I wish I was:
      not lazy
      rich
      in California
      swimming
      blond
      5'4" tall
      not fat
      on my own
      happy
      at a party
      just quiet and feeling good

(name withheld)
JOURNAL

"If I had it all to do over again, I'd . . ." Any regrets? It's a rare person who hasn't.

I can't wait to get out of this school! I keep telling myself that if I can just hang on a little while longer then I can get out of here for the whole summer. The school itself isn't what I hate but I cannot digest the kids here. I'd like to get away for the summer but I was away all last summer and my mother would throw a fit if I even mentioned going away. I keep thinking what a good thing it would be if I could just move away and start over someplace else where nobody knows me, but I got to thinking I realize that wouldn't be an answer because I'd only be running away from my problems and eventually I'm gonna have to face them and find a practical solution to them.

I just read this over and I sound like a horribly mixed-up, unsure little girl. I'm not, I'm really fortunate! I have a good mother and pretty good sisters, a half way decent home. I've got fairly good clothes—not the newest most expensive wardrobe in town but not the worst either. I've never really wanted anything. There are so many people so much worse off than I'll ever dream of being, I should be thankful and even if I don't sound it—I am.

I'm trying very hard to adopt a carefree attitude but I'm not doing so well. I worry so much about what other people think about me it's unreal. I've got all the ideas of how a person with a carefree attitude should act but I just can't apply them to myself.

Kathy Shiels
JOURNAL

IT TOOK ME FIFTEEN YEARS TO DISCOVER I HAD NO TALENT FOR WRITING, BUT I COULDN'T GIVE IT UP BECAUSE BY THAT TIME I WAS TOO FAMOUS.

Robert Benchley

Hateful, the writer who talks about and exploits what he has never experienced. But be careful, a murderer is not the best man to talk of crime. (But isn't he the best man to talk of *his* crime? Even that is not certain.) Essential to imagine a certain distance between creation and the deed. The true artist stands midway between what he imagines and what he does. He is the one who is "capable of." He could be what he describes, experience what he writes. The mere act would limit him; he would be the one who has acted.

Albert Camus
NOTEBOOKS, 1942-1951

If I should write an honest diary, what should I say? Alas, that life has halfness, shallowness. I have almost completed thirty-nine years, and I have not yet adjusted my relation to my fellows on the planet, or to my own work. Always too young or too old, I do not justify myself; how can I satisfy others?

Ralph Waldo Emerson
JOURNAL

78

The seance is to be held in a spacious, comfortable room. You all seat yourselves around a large circular table. The medium suggests that in order to get in the right mood a little singing might be in order. One of the sitters goes to the piano and begins to play some familiar hymns. The group joins in singing enthusiastically, and expectation builds. After a few hymns the medium announces that she is ready.

Now the seance proper is about to begin. The gaslights are turned down, and a screen is set in front of the fire, so that the room becomes very dark. You cannot make out the features of the person seated next to you, and you cannot see the medium at all. You have been told that the darkness is necessary, for the spirits do not like bright lights.

You are instructed to place your hands flat on the table, with your thumbs touching one another. The little fingers of each hand are touching the little fingers of the persons sitting on each side of you. After what seems like an interminable period of absolute silence, a number of astonishing things begin to happen.

First you hear strange noises, knocks, and raps coming from various parts of the room. Then the table upon which you and the other sitters have your hands begins to rise and rock back and forth. It rocks with such force that you have to struggle to keep your hands on top of it, and you press down very hard because the table feels as though it is going to fly away.

Above your head and behind your back various musical instruments—tambourines, horns, and guitars—begin to play mysteriously. A cold breeze suddenly chills you, though before you sat down you were quite sure that all the windows and doors were securely closed. The air now smells perfumed. Something drops into your lap, and the shock startles you into jumping up, and you almost scream. (Later, after the lights are turned on again, you discover what was dropped into your lap was only a bunch of flowers. Such objects, usually flowers or jewelry, which appear in the seance room, apparently from nowhere, are called "apports.")

After taking your seat again, and recovering a bit from the shock of having something dropped into your lap, you feel something else strange. It feels like someone is tugging at your garments under the table. Near where the medium is sitting you see a glowing object peek up over the edge of the table. It is a luminescent hand, but a tiny one like a child's hand. Abruptly the hand is pulled back and everything is in darkness again.

Daniel Cohen
IN SEARCH OF GHOSTS

3/5/59 Morning

In a motel in Winston-Salem: I woke up early and went out to have breakfast at seven-thirty, then returned to my room about eight-thirty and lay down. As I relaxed, the vibrations came and then an impression of movement. Shortly thereafter, I stopped, and the first thing I saw was a boy walking along and tossing a baseball in the air and catching it. A quick shift, and I saw a man trying to put something into the back seat of a car, a large sedan. The thing was an awkward-looking device that I interpreted to be a small car with wheels and electric motor. The man twisted and turned the device and finally got it into the back seat of the car and slammed the door. Another quick shift, and I was standing beside a table. There were people sitting around the table, and dishes covered it. One person was dealing what looked like large white playing cards around to the others at the table. I thought it strange to play cards at a table so covered with dishes, and wondered about the overlarge size and whiteness of the cards. Another quick shift, and I was over city streets, about five hundred feet high, looking for "home." Then I spotted the radio tower, and remembered that the motel was close to the tower, and almost instantly I was back in my body. I sat up and looked around. Everything seemed normal.

Robert A. Monroe
JOURNEYS OUT OF THE BODY

I had written much about out-of-body travel, or astral projection, and had come during my research to realize that there is no doubt of its authenticity. Apparently astral projections occur to a great many people. While one is asleep, or in a completely relaxed state, or possibly when under anesthesia, or in various other conditions, his conscious mind may actually leave his body and soar up, up, and away. It could then happen that he may look down from the ceiling at his body on the bed and suspect that he might have died. If such things occur often, unless knowing that others experience them, he may begin to wonder if he is not a candidate for a straitjacket. Eventually, they say, one becomes used to such goings-on if they happen to him often enough. There are many persons who have learned that they can have such unorthodox adventures at will; even some of my friends do it.

The reason we can be sure these events are not merely subjective is that on occasion someone has been seen elsewhere while his body was, in fact, at home asleep in bed. He has been recognized and identified at this distant site, for the spiritual body in which his consciousness was traveling looked exactly like the physical. It may appear fragile and misty to the beholder; at other times it looks so solid and material that it is taken for the actual physical person. The consciousness of this astral traveler is usually aware of where he is going and what he is doing, and he sometimes returns with knowledge he could have no normal way to learn. There have also been reciprocal cases where the traveler was cognizant of being seen when out of his body and then later had this confirmed.

Susy Smith
CONFESSIONS OF A PSYCHIC

memorabilia n. pl. (L *memorabilis* memorable) 1. things worth remembering or recording; noteworthy matters or events. . . .

If you're hesitant about writing about close friends or important events, emotions, and ideas for fear that someone will read your journal and be offended or ridicule you, try writing in code about these things. Invent pseudonyms for the people who appear in your journal.

Francois Colos

The code-writing of 1881

Page 1 of her visit to Hunt & Roskell, beginning 'Friday November 4/81. We went to Hunt & Roskles . . .'

Note. The lines under H and R indicate capitals, also the name Roskell is wrongly spelt. In the second line she has added the letter *l* to the word silver.

Sit on your windowsill, the branch of a tree, or someplace where you can see people without being seen yourself. Spend about thirty minutes recording what you see.

I worked for Linda Jean throughout my seventh grade year. But that spring and summer Raymond tried farming again, and I was only able to help her on weekends. When I entered eighth grade the following fall we were poorer than ever. Raymond had worse luck with the farm than the year before, so we weren't able to buy any new school clothes. I had added so much meat to my bones that I could squeeze into only two of my old school dresses. They were so tight I was embarrassed to put them on. I had gotten new jeans for the field that summer, so I started wearing them to school two and three days a week. But I continued to fill out so fast that even my jeans got too tight. I got so many wolf whistles from the boys in the class that the faster girls started wearing jeans that were even tighter than mine. When the high school boys started talking about how fine those eighth grade girls were, the high school girls started wearing tight jeans too. I had started a blue jeans fad.

Anne Moody
COMING OF AGE IN MISSISSIPPI

The hero is a man with lofty aspirations whose meanest daily act is impregnated with the drive for immortality.

Akbar Del Piombo

I decline to accept the end of man. It is easy enough to say that man is immortal simply because he will endure: that when the last ding-dong of doom has clanged and faded from the last worthless rock hanging tideless in the last red and dying evening, that even then there will still be one more sound: that of his puny inexhaustible voice, still talking. I refuse to accept this. I believe that man will not merely endure: he will prevail. He is immortal, not because he alone among creatures has an inexhaustible voice, but because he has a soul, a spirit capable of compassion and sacrifice and endurance. The poet's, the writer's, duty is to write about these things. It is his privilege to help man endure by lifting his heart, by reminding him of the courage and honor and hope and pride and compassion and pity and sacrifice which have been the glory of his past. The poet's voice need not merely be the record of man, it can be one of the props, the pillars to help him endure and prevail.

William Faulkner

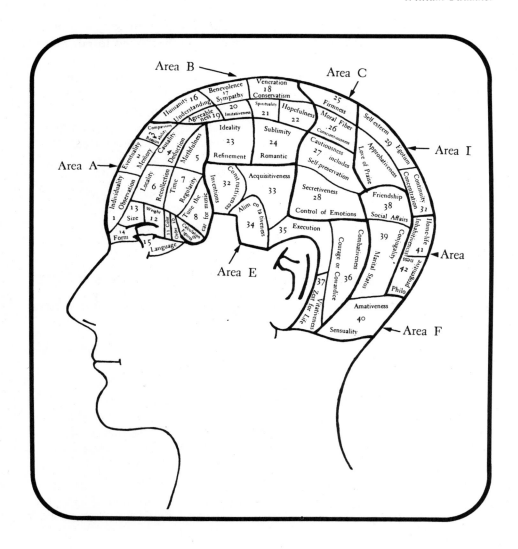

Of the Growth of Man

A man at three years will have reached the half of his height.
A woman of the same size as a man will weigh less than he does.
A dead woman lies face downwards in water, a man the opposite way.

Leonardo Da Vinci
THE NOTEBOOKS OF LEONARDO DA VINCI

What a piece of work is man!
How noble in reason!
How infinite in faculties!
In form and moving how express and admirable!
In action how like an angel!
In apprehension how like a god!
The beauty of the world, the paragon of animals!

William Shakespeare
HAMLET

I hate mankind, for I think myself one of the best of them, and I
know how bad I am.

Samuel Johnson

"Where did you go for your vacation?" asked the tall man waiting
for an elevator in the Smithsonian Institute.
"Cayman Islands," replied the second.
"Where on earth are the Cayman Islands?" the first inquired.
"I've no idea," said the second, "We flew."

R. Buckminster Fuller

Make comparisons. Compare this day with an earlier one; a person just met or observed with one you've known for a while; your present self with your self some time in the past.

Brooding

The sadness of our lives.
We will never be good enough to each other,
to our parents and friends.
We go along like old sailing ships,
loaded with food and drink for a long voyage,
self-sufficient, without any outside contact
with the world.
        The truth faces me
all the time. We are in a world
in which nobody listens to anybody,
in which we do as we please
until we are stopped by others.
We live our whole lives as in a husk,
which keeps us separate from any influence.
While those who reflect the influence
of others are either idiots, or people
who never gained consciousness.

                      David Ignatow

Don't take everything for granted. A little skepticism is healthy. On the other hand, don't overdo your dubiousness; there are some things that we have to take on faith.

"I have shaken hands with a great many friends," he said, "but there are some things I want to know which no one seems able to explain. I cannot understand how the Government sends a man out to fight us, as it did General Miles, and then breaks his word. Such a Government has something wrong about it. . . . I do not understand why nothing is done for my people. I have heard talk and talk, but nothing is done. Good words do not last long until they amount to something. Words do not pay for my dead people. They do not pay for my country, now overrun by white men. They do not protect my father's grave. . . . Good words will not give me back my children. . . . Good words will not give my people good health and stop them from dying. Good words will not get my people a home where they can live in peace and take care of themselves. I am tired of talk that comes to nothing. It makes my heart sick when I remember all the good words and all the broken promises. . . ."

remarks by Chief Joseph
THE NEZ PERCE INDIANS AND THE OPENING OF THE NORTHWEST

The upper castes regard us as the dirty peoples. Dirty is the right word; it accurately describes what the Hindu thinks of us. Of course we must be disgusting objects to him; of course we often turn his stomach. He washes his garments *every day;* we come into his presence in coat, vest and breeches that have never been in the wash since they left the tailor's hands; they are stale with ancient sweat, tobacco smoke and so on. No doubt he says "Ugh!" and retches; but his feelings are not allowed to show outside, for he is a courteous being.

You say the Hindus are unspeakably indecent in their language—the grown people and the children alike? If they so earnestly desire to be cleanly, why do they do that?

Because according to their standard such things are not objectionable. Also, according to their standard lying is not a sin. They all lie and think it no evil. Another thing, you have noticed from the car windows that they publicly and without embarrassment indulge in various habits which to us are forbidden. By their standard this is no offense. In Japan formerly both sexes bathed naked in public. The newly arrived white people were disgusted. The innocent Japanese said—"What dirty minds these white people have." By their social creed all the details of the body were worthy of respect since the gods made them and no detail of it is contemptible or indecent. Each race determines for itself what indecencies are. Nature knows no indecencies; man invents them.

Mark Twain
NOTEBOOK

Listen to children. There's a lot to be gained from this, not the least of which is that it's a good idea to learn to listen to people, period. But children, perhaps because they know so little, have a way of asking the big questions of life—Where does the rain come from? Why do people die? And yet their lives aren't simple, as some romantic adults like to think. There is as much care, as much emotion, as much thought, in a child's life as there is in an adult's.

In the speech of children you may find something of yourself. You may be reminded of things you did and felt as a child. You may become aware of changes in yourself since you were a child—and you may find changes you like and some you don't. If you're very good at listening, you'll stop thinking of these people as "children" and find instead that here is a group of individual people, each one unique, who happen to be young. Try to get down in your journal as many worthwhile ideas from children as you can. Don't rephrase them in your own words—that's you talking, not the child—try to write them as direct quotations, as accurately as you can. Keep your reactions separate from the child's words.

Consider the lilies of the field, how they grow; they toil not, neither do they spin: and yet I say unto you that even Solomon in all his glory was not arrayed like one of these.

The Gospel According to St. Matthew

89

Child mine workers

Play is the highest expression of human development in the child, for it alone is the free expression of what is in the child's soul. It is the purest and most spiritual product of the child and at the same time it is a type and copy of human life at all stages and in all relations.

Friedrich Froebel
THE EDUCATION OF MAN

Dr. David Premack of the University of California at Santa Barbara has taught a chimpanzee to "talk" to him in English, or at least a language based on English. The chimpanzee, Sarah, communicates by putting plastic markers of different colors into line to form "sentences." Sarah can ask and answer questions, obey "written" commands, and understand some grammar. She has even mastered conditional sentences of the if-X-happens-then-Y-will-happen type.

In the Middle Ages, serfs had a homemade weapon which they learned to use with devastating power, even against knights on horseback. (Serfs were not always docile!) This weapon was a staff which had been hewn from a tree. The plural of staff was *staves*. Used offensively, the staves literally *staved off* defeat. When sports commentators talk about the Harvard football team's staving off defeat on its two-yard line, few people realize what the precise image is that the phrase is supposed to bring to mind. The semantic movement is as follows:

1. From noun to verb
2. From verb to metaphor
3. From metaphor to "buried metaphor"

André Malraux, French novelist, art critic, and minister of culture in the De Gaulle regime, has said that all art is the "art of the metaphor." Language has been described as a graveyard of metaphors. A metaphor is "dead" or "buried" when it no longer evokes a striking picture in the imagination.

Sidney Shanker
SEMANTICS: THE MAGIC OF WORDS

In a very real sense, the 20th century poses an unprecedented problem for language. The mass media—newspapers, magazines, books, movies, radio, and television—consume words and burn them out at an alarming rate. In the past, hardy words had a life span of hundreds of years. Some words today, particularly superlatives, last but a few years! The single word *awful* is a good example. In Shakespeare's time it was a very strong word. When Hamlet sees his father's ghost, he experiences awe; his hair stands on end; his heart knocks at his ribs. *Awe* means "dread" plus "veneration." Today, waiting a few minutes to make a phone call is "awful." Advertisements for some Hollywood movies have consumed, burnt out, such strong words as *fantastic, colossal, supercolossal, spectacular,* and *greatest.*

Sidney Shanker
SEMANTICS: THE MAGIC OF WORDS

Doodle in words. Jot down words as they come to you. Let one word suggest the next. Play with rhymes. Contrast harsh sounds and soft sounds. Put down words whose sounds match the sounds around you.

Birthplace Revisited

I stand in the dark light in the dark street
and look up at my window, I was born there.
The lights are on; other people are moving about.
I am with raincoat; cigarette in mouth,
hat over eye, hand on gat.
I cross the street and enter the building.
The garbage cans haven't stopped smelling.
I walk up the first flight; Dirty Ears
aims a knife at me . . .
I pump him full of lost watches.

Gregory Corso

Unfortunately, many things have been omitted which should have been recorded in our journal; for though we made it a rule to set down all our experiences therein, yet such a resolution is very hard to keep, for the important experience rarely allows us to remember such obligation, and so indifferent things get recorded, while that is frequently neglected. It is not easy to write in a journal what interests us at any time, because to write it is not what interests us.

Henry David Thoreau
A WEEK ON THE CONCORD AND MERRIMACK RIVERS

What pleased you today? Search your memory until you find something, no matter how small.

What irritated you today? Search your memory until you find something, no matter how small.

Dinner

Sir, respect your dinner, idolize it, enjoy it properly. You will be by many hours in the week, many weeks in the year, and many years in your life, the happier if you do.

Don't tell me it is not worthy of a man. All a man's senses are worthy of employment, and should be cultivated as a duty. The senses are the arts. What glorious feasts does Nature prepare for your eye in animal form, in landscape and in painting! Are you to put out your eyes and not see? What royal dishes does her bounty provide for you in the shape of poetry, music, whether windy or wiry, notes of the human voice, or ravishing songs of birds! Are you to stuff your ears with cotton, and vow that the sense of hearing is unmanly? —You obstinate dolt you! No, surely; nor must you be so absurd as to fancy that the art of eating is in any way less worthy than the other two. You like your dinner, man! Never be ashamed to say so. If you don't like your victuals, pass on to the next article; but remember that every man who has been worth a fig in this world as poet, painter, or musician, has had a good appetite, and a good taste.

William Makepeace Thackeray

At approximately 10:45 A.M. the radio blasts me out of bed with David Rose's "The Stripper." Groggy, I stumble down the hall to watch my mother and father doing bumps and grinds in the middle of the living room rug. My grandmother emerges from the guest room, cataractic eyes gleaming frog-like behind magnifying glasses, and beams, "That's my boy."

I return to my bedroom and emerge later fully dressed. I proceed to the kitchen, collect my food, and sit down next to my sister, which is as far from her as I can get, and proceed to be sick.

Watching my sister eat is something as disheartening as Napoleon at Waterloo. She has grapefruit every morning. That I don't object to, if she'd only eat it normally. Other people put sugar on theirs and that's it, but not her. She sprinkles it with brown sugar and then pours maple syrup on it. Yechh.

Usually by the time she has finished this operation, my brother has sneezed in his Rice Krispies, showering them all over everything and everyone. My sister screams, "What's wrong with you? You've gotten Rice Krispies in my grapefruit. Do you want me to catch something?"

Frankly, I wish she would catch something, like the bubonic plague. But she's immune to everything. She didn't even get colic when she was a baby.

Robin Kascenska
JOURNAL

FROM THE PRESENT POINT OF VIEW, CHILD REARING MAY BE REGARDED AS AN EDUCATIONAL PROCESS IN WHICH THE CHILD IS TAUGHT WHAT GAMES TO PLAY AND HOW TO PLAY THEM.

ERIC BERNE
GAMES PEOPLE PLAY

The possibility of controlling whole nations through drugs is no fantasy. Chemicals could be put into the water people drink, the air they breathe, the food they eat. They could be made hostile, docile, or helpless with glee, actually laughing so long and so hard that they couldn't do anything else and soon become weak with hunger and exhaustion. Experiments with animals have shown that this is easily possible, and more than one scientist has already suggested putting a birth-control chemical into the water of overpopulated countries.

Some babies could be drugged from birth with chemicals that would limit their brain development and improve their muscular development. Others could be given drugs to improve the brain. The one group would grow up to be the workers, the other the leaders. . . .

For the purpose of teaching and instruction is to bring ever more *out* of man rather than to put more *into* him; for that which can get *into* man we already know and possess as the property of mankind. On the other hand, what yet is to come *out* of mankind, what human nature is yet to develop, that we do not yet know.

Friedrich Froebel

The frame of mind that makes things so beautiful always widens into hatred when I think of someone I dislike, for example our Professor of Design who was at the German school in the few miserable years I attended it.

He prided himself upon the faultless discipline in his classroom. No boy ever asked to step out; the hour there, which might have been one of few happy ones, began with the wordless entrance of the pupils, at the minute before the hour, after they had formed themselves into a column of two rows outside the door. We marched in, turned sharply at our assigned benches, and sat down erect, with both hands, palm down, in front of us.

The Professor stepped up to his desk and tapped with a pencil. This meant to put pencil number one, the soft graphite, on the table; the next tap brought pencil number two, the harder; the next tap, the eraser; then the dust cloth, and after that the drawing block. Then he ran around; pencils were held up to show that they were properly sharpened; the Primus of the class was allowed to bring out of a box a wooden sphere for each student to draw.

This evil teacher ruined whatever free talent there was in his class, helped us to hate paper and pencils, and most of all himself and his room and the building he was in.

Ludwig Bemelmans

memento n. (L *meminisse* to remember) . . . 2. anything serving as a reminder, warning, or souvenir.

Collect interesting and unusual place names. You might want to look some of them up in a book such as *American Place Names*.

Deliberately write some entries without using complete sentences. Just write words and phrases connected with dashes or empty space. You may find this especially effective for getting lots of action down quickly or for recording a chaos of ideas and emotions.

Stinging eyes—Coke taste in my mouth—itchy—poison
ivy—tired—can't think of anything—too quiet—voices downstairs—cars
outside—shoes on sidewalk—walkers talking—walking and talking—a talk
walk—let's go for a walk and talk—I need to talk—I need to talk to
someone—I need to scratch my knee—my knee needed that—let's talk
about my knee—let's walk and talk about my knee—a knee-talk
walk—and scratch—a knee-scratch knee-talk walk.

Gary Hopper
JOURNAL

A
SOUL IS AN EXPENSIVE THING
TO MAINTAIN

**Describe a ceremony, such as a wedding or an inauguration. Pay
close attention to the language that is used as part of the ceremony.**

Are Members permitted to wear hats on the floor of Congress?
Until 1837, it was permissible for Congressmen to wear hats during
sessions, after the fashion of members of Britain's Parliament. Since then
Members of Congress have been prohibited from covering their heads
until after leaving the legislative Chamber.

OUR AMERICAN GOVERNMENT: WHAT IS IT? HOW DOES IT FUNCTION?

"Mr. Sheridan," said I, "I have thought a good deal upon
education. I see so many difficulties that I despair of finding a good
method. I think of our existence here as a jest; it is not intended that we
should do much here that has any purpose; and therfore we must just
get through it the best way we can."

James Boswell
LONDON JOURNAL
[adapted slightly]

96

The Three Laws of Thermodynamics

1. You can't win.
2. You can't break even.
3. You can't get out of the game.

Describe a surprise.

Cartoon by
Ton Smits.

TO : SAC, PHILADELPHIA

FROM : SAC, NEWARK (157-5183) (P)

DATE : 2/22/71

SUBJECT : CHANGED

DENISE E. BRUSKIN, aka

DENNIS BRUSKIN

RM

Title marked Changed to reflect the name DENISE E. BRUSKIN from Livingston College records.

Re Portland letter to Bureau, 1/8/71, captioned, "REVOLUTIONARY PEOPLES CONSTITUTIONAL CONVENTION ORGANIZED BY THE BLACK PANTHER PARTY".

Relet, a copy of which was designated for Philadelphia, contained the name of the subject and identified him as being from Livingston College, LPO 11373, New Brunswick, New Jersey.

On 2/4/71, ROBERT BUNKER, Assistant Chief, Rutgers Campus Patrol, an established and reliable source (Protect), advised that there is no indication that the above-listed organization is active on either the Rutgers or Livingston College campuses. BUNKER advised Livingston College is a division of Rutgers University. He advised, however, that a DENISE E. BRUSKIN, a resident of House 27, Livingston Post Office 11373, is a permanent resident of 4015 Brunswick Avenue, Drexel Hill, Pa. She is a freshman at Livingston College. BUNKER advised he would attempt to obtain additional background data on BRUSKIN.

LEADS:

PHILADELPHIA

1. *At Drexel Hill, Pennsylvania:* will obtain background data on subject from high school records and contact with sources.

2. Will conduct credit and identification checks for subject.

3. Will determine from sources whether subject is known to be associated with BPP or similar New Left activities.

At New Brunswick, New Jersey: Will maintain contact with Assistant Chief ROBERT BUNKER for information on BRUSKIN.

Massive Voter Registration Campaign. Building in Illinois Black Communities

The Black Panther Party brought three busloads of students to City Hall, in downtown Chicago, where they were registered to vote. This is only the beginning of the drive to educate and register people to progressively use our collective voting power.

The reactionary politicians have had the gall to say that they speak for the oppressed masses of the people, while constantly ignoring our needs. The oppressed masses are in turn beginning to silence the corrupticians through positive and concrete organization.

ALL POWER TO THE PEOPLE
Illinois State Chapter
Black Panther Party

THE BLACK PANTHER

The world is full of momentous events. Earth-shaking news may not be made on your block or even in your city, but it affects you nonetheless. In your journal, react to the big events and issues of the day. Don't be afraid of your opinion. No one will see it but you.

Speculate on what a present event may mean in the future. Make predictions. This is fun any time, but especially so at the start of a new year.

Include your reactions to a movie, a TV program, a book, a conversation, or whatever. There's no need to write an essay (unless you wish to). Just put down your feelings.

One of these children of twelve thought up a questionnaire (or more precisely he pinched this questionnaire from a slightly older cousin, and several of them amused themselves by filling it out).

Here are the questions, some of them inept and others rather significant. I am copying faithfully:

1. What is your motto?
2. Who is your best friend?
3. What is the dominant trait of your character?

4. What vocation would you like to have?
5. How would you prefer to die?
6. What is your favorite book?
7. What real-life hero do you prefer?
8. Where do you most like to be?
9. What is your idea of happiness?
10. What is your idea of unhappiness?
11. What is the quality that you prefer?
    Etc. . . .

I notice without surprise that detective novels and the heroes of aviation are at the top.

But this is odder: out of fourteen children questioned, four answer "marriage" to question No. 10: "What is your idea of unhappiness?" Only two attach the idea of marriage to happiness. . . .

André Gide
THE JOURNALS OF ANDRÉ GIDE

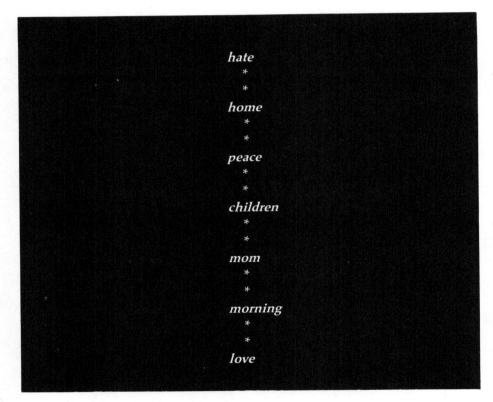

London Bridge is in Arizona.
The Queen Mary is in California.
Come to Britain while it lasts.

Every once in a while, prime yourself to notice everything remarkable during the day. Odd things. Ridiculous things. Real things that are strangely out of the ordinary. Look for them everywhere, anywhere, as you go through the day. List them all in your journal at night.

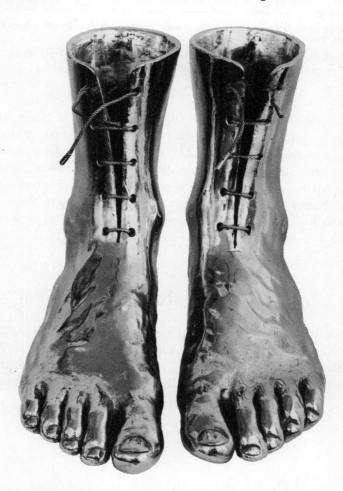

101

POPULATION THROUGH HISTORY

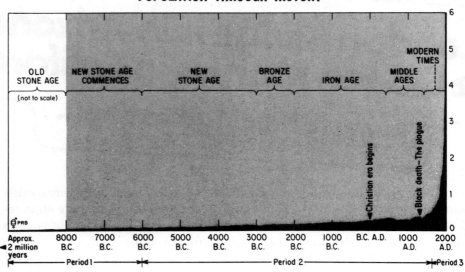

Source: Population Reference Bureau, Inc. "How Many People Have Ever Lived on Earth?", *Population Bulletin*, Vol. XVIII, No. 1.

Man's numbers reached a half billion by the year 1650 A.D.; at present rates population is increasing by one billion in a dozen years.

Within the next generation or so, the population of Japan will stop growing and begin to decrease, if the trend in that country continues. Of all the major countries of the world, only in Japan has the population growth rate been steadily decreasing, the result of voluntary controls.

Many Japanese sociologists believe that widespread interest in birthcontrol began back in 1918, when the country was rocked by bloody riots over the high price and low supply of rice. The Japanese seem to have seen it as a warning . . .

Busiest Railroad

The world's most crowded rail system is the Japanese National Railways, which in 1971 carried 16,495,000 passengers daily. Professional pushers are employed in the Tokyo subway to squeeze in passengers before the doors can be closed. Among articles reported lost in the crush in 1970 were 419,929 umbrellas, 250,630 eyeglasses and hats, 172,106 shoes, and also an assortment of false teeth and artificial eyeballs.

GUINNESS BOOK OF WORLD RECORDS

Them Hors D'Oeuvres

How about Them Hors D'Oeuvres,
Ain't they sweet?
Little piece a cheese,
Little piece a meat.

Mason Williams
THE MASON WILLIAMS READING MATTER

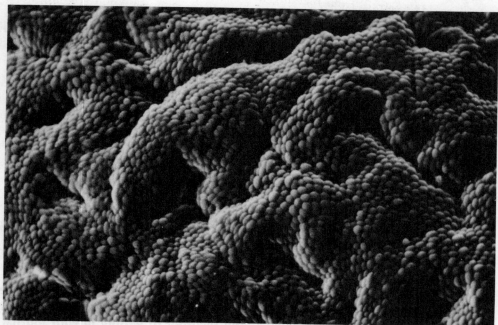

Micrograph of stomach lining.

What's on your mind? Have you ever had people ask you that? Some time when you are not doing anything else, jot down everything that comes into your head. Spend at least fifteen minutes on this.

My longing to talk to someone became so intense that somehow or other I took it into my head to choose Peter.

Sometimes . . . I tried to think of an excuse to stay in his room and get him talking, without it being too noticeable, and my chance came yesterday. Peter has a mania for crossword puzzles at the moment and hardly does anything else. I helped him with them and we soon sat opposite each other at his little table, he on the chair and me on the divan.

It gave me a queer feeling each time I looked into his deep blue eyes, and . . . I noticed his shy manner and it made me feel very gentle; I couldn't refrain from meeting those dark eyes again and again, and with my whole heart I almost beseeched him: Oh, tell me, what is going on inside you, oh, can't you look beyond this ridiculous chatter?

But the evening passed and nothing happened, except that I told him about blushing—naturally not what I have written, but just so that he would become more sure of himself as he grew older.

When I lay in bed and thought over the whole situation, I found it far from encouraging · · ·

Anne Frank
THE DIARY OF A YOUNG GIRL

Try using your journal to work out a problem that has been bothering you. Hold a dialogue with yourself and give yourself advice.

Some writers use a tape recorder for getting down what they have to say. If you have access to a tape recorder, use it to record one of your journal entries. Compare using a tape recorder to writing in your journal. What are the advantages and disadvantages of each method?

A London Thoroughfare. 2 A. M.

They have watered the street,
It shines in the glare of the lamps,
Cold, white lamps,
And lies
Like a slow-moving river,
Barred with silver and black.
Cabs go down it,
One,
And then another,
Between them I hear the shuffling of feet.
Tramps doze on the window-ledges,
Night-walkers pass along the sidewalks.
The city is squalid and sinister,
With the silver-barred street in the midst,
Slow-moving,
A river leading nowhere.

Opposite my window,
The moon cuts,
Clear and round,
Through the plum-coloured night.
She cannot light the city:
It is too bright.
It has white lamps,
And glitters coldly.

I stand in the window and watch the moon.
She is thin and lustreless,
But I love her.
I know the moon,
And this is an alien city.

Amy Lowell

If you want to capture *this* moment for your journal, you're wasting your time to write about it in general terms. In my own journal for one year I found six entries that read, "A good day," or "I felt great today," several that said "Bad day," and one that read "A ROTTEN DAY." What happened on those days? I don't know; they're lost, and I'm curious to know what made me feel so good or so bad then.

You'd do better, in the eyes of your future self, to write even one specific phrase than to fill pages with abstractions about how you feel. The abstractions have their use, but capturing a moment is not it.

At this point, steam issues from the stew pot. You reduce the heat to dead-low or thereabouts (taking care not to turn the stove off in the process), stir the compound a couple of times, inhale appreciatively and replace the cover. While dinner simmers toward fruition you empty two ounces of dehydrated peaches and a little water into the small cooking pot and put it ready for breakfast, up alongside the pack. Then you jot down a few thoughts in your notebook, stir the stew and sample it, find the beans are not quite soft yet. So you study the map and worry a bit about the morning's route, put map and pen and pencil and eyeglasses and thermometer into the bedside boots, take off your shorts and slide halfway down into the mummy bag out of the wind, and stir the stew again and find all ready. You pour-and-spoon out a cupful, leaving the balance on the stove because the wind is blowing distinctly cool now. And then, leaning comfortably back against the pack and watching the sky and the black peaks meld, you eat, cupful by cupful, your dinner. . . .

Colin Fletcher
THE COMPLETE WALKER

Change all the verb tenses in some previously-written journal entry. What effect does this change have on the meaning of what you wrote originally?

106

Try writing something in any form you wish, with any tone from serious to ridiculous, using at least ten of the following words. Change the form of the words if you want or need to.

rakish	tailor	vair	swannery
lithography	wit	investigable	video
wineskin	redoubtable	fiancé	professorate
flash	oppression	distend	nucleon
distaste	integrate	oyster catcher	lap

FORSYTHIA

As the cold water gushed forth, filling the mug, I spelled "w-a-t-e-r" in Helen's free hand. The word coming so close upon the sensation of cold water rushing over her hand seemed to startle her. She dropped the mug and stood as one transfixed. A new light came into her face. She spelled "water" several times. Then she dropped on the ground and asked for its name and pointed to the pump and the trellis, and suddenly turning round she asked for my name.

from letter written by Anne Sullivan
HELEN KELLER: THE STORY OF MY LIFE

Like other animals, man develops, is born, grows, reproduces, and dies. Like other animals, he eats, digests, eliminates, respires, locomotes. He bends the qualities of nature to his own ends, but he is as fully subject to nature's laws as is any other animal and is no more capable of changing them. He lives in biological communities and has a niche and an ecology, just as do robins and earthworms. Let us not forget those aspects of man's nature. But let us also remember that man stands upright, builds and makes as never was built or wrought before, speaks and may speak truth or a lie, worships and may worship honestly or falsely, looks to the stars and into the mud, remembers his past and predicts his future, and writes (perhaps at too great length) about his own nature.

George Gaylord Simpson

Man and the animals are merely a passage and channel for food, a tomb for other animals, a haven for the dead, gaining life by the death of others, a coffer full of corruption.

Leonardo Da Vinci
THE NOTEBOOKS OF LEONARDO DA VINCI

If one were to hazard a guess, it might not be too far wrong to say that during the time of the great hunting cultures (approximately 25,000 years ago) man was the happiest he has ever been. For man, it seems, was a natural hunting creature, a born predator. He fit into his ecology and knew his environment thoroughly. He was doing a job to which he naturally was fitted and something that he enjoyed doing. It was a simple life of direct action and the only complexities he faced were the tribal and ritualistic practices that would vary from tribe to tribe. The yearning for this kind of uncluttered life is still with us. Men still seek it by the millions, embarking upon hunting and fishing trips, going camping or hiking, engaging in such activities as bird watching or hunting rocks and fossils. All of these activities serve as an excuse to cut away for a time from the tangled matrix of present-day life and to get next to nature, to enjoy the kind of environment that one's ancient ancestors lived with from day to day, and to experience once again the sense of freedom and of quiet that goes with living close to nature, even for an hour or two.

Clifford D. Simak

> ## Where would you like to go?

A fountain breaks out in the wilderness, but that fountain cares not whether any man comes to fetch water or not; a fresh and fit gale blows upon the sea, but it cares not whether the mariners hoist sail or no; a rose blows in your garden, but it calls you not to smell it.

John Donne

If your mind had weather of its own, how would you report the state of your mental meteorology today?

Long ago, in quieter times, people had confidants, trustworthy friends to whom they could confide their desires, their sins, their shortcomings, their private triumphs, their troubles, their tragedies. Some people don't seem to confide in anyone so completely any more. You can trust, confide in, and confess to your journal.

---

progris riport martch 3
Dr. Strauss says I shoud rite down what I think and remembir and evrey thing that happins to me from now on. I dont no why but he says its importint so they will see if they can use me. I hope they use me becaus Miss Kinnian says mabye they can make me smart. I want to be smart. My name is Charlie Gordon I werk in Donners bakery where Mr Donner gives me 11 dollers a week and bred or cake if I want. I am 32 yeres old and next munth is my birthday. I tolld dr Strauss and perfesser Nemur I cant rite good but he says it dont matter he says I shud rite just like I talk and like I write compushishens in Miss Kinnians class at the beekmin collidge center for retarted adults where I go to lern 3 times a week on my time off. Dr. Strauss says to rite a lot evrything I think and evrything that happins to me but I cant think anymor because I have nothing to rite so I will close for today. . . yrs truly Charlie Gordon.

Daniel Keyes
FLOWERS FOR ALGERNON

As your journal grows and becomes more important to you, try carrying an auxiliary journal, a small pocket notebook, with you wherever you go. Don't worry about looking like a late-show movie reporter; you can find private moments to make notes on interesting occurrences and

thoughts. Transfer these jottings, in expanded form perhaps, into your journal when you have time.

A dunghill at a distance sometimes smells like musk, & a dead dog like elder-flowers.

Samuel Taylor Coleridge
NOTEBOOKS

Make a list of the things you have lost or misplaced. Put a check in front of those that you wish you still had. Add to the list any items that have mysteriously disappeared; elaborate on the circumstances if you like.

Supplement your written entries with photographs, postcards, and souvenirs.

Often we overhear other people's conversations. There are places, sitting beside someone on a bus or at the beach, sitting in front of someone at the movies, waiting in line, where we can hardly avoid it. Take advantage of these times. The people are unknown to you, and they'll remain anonymous in your journal, so writing about them and what they say can't do them any harm. What is this person like? What does he have to say? What does he think about? Worry about? What pleases him? What does his life seem to be like? How is he like you? How is he different?

Little Rock, Ark.—A national data bank with records of 300,000 migrant children is being set up here. . . .

The system is designed to aid the rapid placement of children in school. Using a WATS (Wide Area Telephone Service) line, a school official will be able to call the Little Rock center free of charge and get the school and health records of the child. With this system, "the child can be placed immediately," according to Joe Miller (no relation to the author), newly appointed director of the Data Bank for Migrant Children.

When asked who had access to the data, Miller replied: "Well, I suppose anyone." Asked if there were any restrictions on the use of the data, he said: "Well, I wouldn't think so."

None of the information in the data bank could be used in a

derogatory way, Miller said. Personal information, such as questions about the family and their moral habits, has been excluded, he explained.

But he said that the file contained an "extensive record of tests and health information," including the child's "strong and weak points" in school.

The data bank is being set up by the federal programs division of the Arkansas Department of Education under a $426,150 grant from the U. S. Office of Education. School and health records of 300,000 children of migrant farm workers will be stored . . . at the University of Arkansas Medical Center. . . .

Data will come from files of "record-transfer forms" maintained by the 47 state directors of migrant education. Beginning this fall, copies of these files will be mailed to Little Rock for keypunching and insertion into the data bank. . . .

According to Miller, the data bank can be updated each time the child moves.

Arthur R. Miller
THE ASSAULT ON PRIVACY

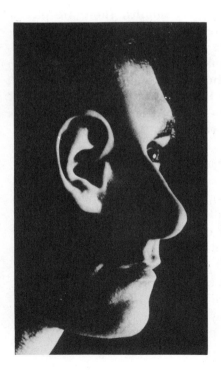

Orange

Today i was looking at an orange
It
Was orange.
But also it was a fake.
Because
Somebody stuck
Needles of flaming color into it.
Real
Oranges are
Usually brown and green but
This
One was
Orange.

Lawrence Dickey
JOURNAL

The tree which moves some to tears of joy is in the eyes of others only a green thing which stands in the way... As a man is, so he sees.

William Blake

The Blindman

The blindman placed
a tulip on his tongue for purple's taste.
Cheek to grass, his green

was rough excitement's sheen
of little whips.
In water to his lips

he named the sea blue and white,
the basin of his tears and fallen beads of sight.
He said: This scarf is red;

I feel the vectors to its thread
that dance down from the sun. I know
the seven fragrances of the rainbow.

I have caressed
the orange hair of flames. Pressed
to my ear,

a pomegranate lets me hear
crimson's flute.
Trumpets tell me yellow. Only ebony is mute.

May Swenson

Choose one color and record all the important occurrences of it this day in your life.

113

Scenes and characters:—A young country fellow, twenty or thereabouts, decently dressed, pained with the toothache. A doctor, passing on horseback, with his black leather saddlebags behind him, a thin, frosty-haired man. Being asked to operate, he looks at the tooth, lances the gum, and the fellow being content to be dealt with on the spot, he seats himself in a chair on the stoop with great heroism. The doctor produces a rusty pair of iron forceps; a man holds the patient's head; the doctor perceives that, it being a difficult tooth to get at, wedged between the two largest in his jaw, he must pull very hard; and the instrument is introduced. A turn of the doctor's hand; the patient begins to utter a cry, but the tooth comes out first, with four prongs. The patient gets up, half amazed, pays the doctor ninepence, pockets the tooth, and the spectators are in glee and admiration.

Nathaniel Hawthorne
AMERICAN NOTEBOOKS

In a squatter camp at the edge of the pea fields. The crop froze this year and the family is destitute. On this morning they had sold the tires from their car to pay for food. She is thirty-two years old.

The old jail in Cambridge was immediately back of Mrs. Kneeland's house. The inmates of the prison were very bad neighbors and used to take delight in pestering Mrs. Kneeland with foul names and profane language. Professor Hedge took great pains to get the nuisance removed, and at last the old jail was pulled down. Someone congratulated Mrs. K. upon her happy deliverance, but found her quite sad at the loss of her stimulus. 'She kind o' missed 'em,' she said.

Ralph Waldo Emerson
NOTEBOOK

Sunday
    I was sitting at the counter in the luncheonette when this old guy on my right starts talking to me. I just sit and drink my coffee and pretend to listen, but he's such a persistent and animated talker that, after a few moments, I find myself listening intently to his stories. He was telling of his experiences as a cab driver during the Depression and seemed to have a very vivid recollection of such long-ago events. I laugh when he relates an incident involving the man who is now our local police chief, a speakeasy that used to be on the outskirts of our town, and a set of car keys lost in a snowbank on a cold, dark night. I even order a second cup of coffee and listen some more, but finally I have to excuse myself. He gives me a big smile and wishes me the best of luck. I step out onto the sidewalk wondering if I'll ever see him again.

Frank Quinlan
JOURNAL

Don't let an unusual person escape your journal. Get something down, a description of him or her or snatches of a conversation.

Exaggerate something that you did. Don't be bashful—really blow it up.

I lay down on the grass, which was very short and soft, where I slept sounder than ever I remember to have done in my life, and, as I reckoned, above nine hours; for when I awaked, it was just daylight. I attempted to rise, but was not able to stir: for as I happened to lie on my back, I found my arms and legs were strongly fastened on each side to the ground; and my hair, which was long and thick, tied down in the same manner. I likewise felt several slender ligatures across my body, from my armpits to my thighs. I could only look upwards, the sun began to grow hot, and the light offended my eyes. I heard a confused noise about me, but, in the posture I lay, could see nothing except the sky. In a little time I felt something alive moving on my left leg, which advancing gently forward over my breast, came almost up to my chin; when, bending my eyes downwards as much as I could, I perceived it to be a human creature not six inches high, with a bow and arrow in his hands, and a quiver at his back.

Jonathan Swift
GULLIVER'S TRAVELS

116

Two separate questions asked in a questionnaire administered to 2,000 young men were: What is the largest (smallest) number of children you would choose to have?

Number of Children	Percentage	
	Largest	Smallest
0	2	8
1	2	32
2	21	48
3	24	6
4	24	1
5	12	–
6	6	–
7	1	–
8 or more	4	–
Missing data	5	5

Jerald G. Bachman and Elizabeth Van Duinen
adapted from YOUTH LOOK AT NATIONAL PROBLEMS

Who am I
to stand and wonder
to wait
while the wheels of fate
slowly grind my life away?
Who am I?

What a nothing I've made of life
the empty words, the coward's plight
to be pushed and passed from hand to hand
never daring to speak, never daring to stand
and the emptiness of my family's eyes
reminds me over and over of lies
of promises and deeds undone
and now again I want to run
but now there is nowhere to run to.

Joe McDonald

> ## THE UNEXAMINED lIFE IS NOT WORTH liVING.
>
> *Socrates*

Imagine a physical problem, such as how to get over a wall that has no gate. List as many approaches to this problem as you can.

March 20, 1865.—Heard that the upper class at the Gymnasium [high school] has been closed because of insubordination. Our young people are detestable and are becoming more and more unmanageable and insolent. Their motto, in the French style, is, "Our master is our enemy." The baby wishes to have the privileges of the young man, and the young man means to keep those of the ill-behaved little boy. This is caused by our system of "democracy" and "equality." From the moment that differences in quality are officially equal to zero in politics, the authority of knowledge, age, and position is bound to disappear. Then the most careless student will treat his masters as equals.

The only antidote to this equalitarianism is military discipline. To the officer's stripes and the guardroom, the dungeon and the firing-squad, there is no reply. . . .

Henri Frédéric Amiel
PRIVATE JOURNAL
[adapted slightly]

✗ ✗ ✗ ✗ ✗

Meditation is an art, the art of fixing one's attention so strongly on one thing that everything else is excluded from the mind. Try it. Pick an idea, an object, or an experience that means something to you and concentrate only on that. Don't let go of it until you've wrung all the thoughts and feelings out of it that you can. Where did it come from? What good is it? What does it mean to you? What has it meant in the past? What significance might it have in the future? What difference does it make? Try to get it all down, all of it.

Keep trying.

118

Few people think more than two or three times a year; I have made an international reputation for myself by thinking two or three times a week.

George Bernard Shaw

April 29

The fact that I have read a lot and that I think and write has never generated in me the conviction that I could teach and guide others. Even in a union meeting of unlearned longshoremen it has never occurred to me that I could tell them what to do. This reluctance to teach and guide is the result not of a lack of confidence in myself but rather of a confidence in the competence of the run-of-the-mill American.

The important point is that the lack of the conviction that I have the ability and the right to teach others marks me as a non-intellectual. For the intellectual is above all a teacher, and considers it his God-given right to tell the ignorant majority what to do. To ignore this teacher complex is to ignore the intellectual's central characteristic, and miss the key to his aspirations and grievances. I am sure that the passion to teach has been a crucial factor in the rise of the revolutionary movements of our time. In most cases when a revolutionary takes over a country he turns it into a vast schoolroom with a population of cowed, captive pupils cringing at his feet. When he speaks the whole country listens.

Eric Hoffer
WRITING AND THINKING ON THE WATERFRONT

Bringing up a child is making him obey, helping him to rise above himself, and teaching him to love and want and do things which he does not spontaneously love or want to do—values which he will someday serve, just as they serve him.

Louis Evely
TRAINING CHILDREN FOR MATURITY

. . . Ask yourself how many of these self-confidence destroyers you may be unwittingly practicing on your child.

(1) Are you babying the child rather than encouraging him to do things for himself?

(2) Are you making his home life tense rather than relaxed?

(3) Are you giving out with more disapproval than praise?

(4) Are you pushing the child beyond his abilities rather than realizing his limitations?

(5) Are you aloof rather than friendly with the child?

(6) Are you riding the child on his weaknesses rather than trying to improve them?

(7) Are you holding up a superior child as an example rather than comparing the child to someone nearer his own abilities?

(8) Are you demanding perfection rather than showing some tolerance?

(9) Are you providing the child with unnecessary worries rather than making him feel secure?

(10) Are you setting an "I can't" example rather than exhibiting self-sufficiency yourself?

(11) Are you overly protecting the child rather than teaching him responsibility?

(12) Are you letting the child withdraw from situations he should be made to face?

B. Von Haller Gilmer
HOW TO HELP YOUR CHILD DEVELOP SUCCESSFULLY

No matter how hard you try to control your child's social life, he is sure to have some friends whom you don't like very well. If you live in a neighborhood where the people are pretty much like yourselves, your peeves may be confined to a few children who displease you in minor ways. People who live in towns are likely to live among their friends and others of similar background, income and standards. Many people in cities live in neighborhoods where a goodly number of the residents differ so widely from themselves that there is little basis for friendship and understanding. Parents who are thus isolated have a much more difficult time fitting their children into the neighborhood with a minimum of friction. In any case, the neighbors' children are never perfect, and we all have to make some effort if we are going to get along with them.

Mollie Stevens Smart and Russell Cook Smart
IT'S A WISE PARENT

Force is the commonest tool of the authority of constraint. The adult, by virtue of his strength and size alone, can impose his will on the young child in a purely physical way. This is the easy and lazy method of control, alike in families, communities or among the nations. But it has difficulties; rebellion is always lurking around the corner. Such rebellion has often been accepted by the parent as inevitable. This rationalization is calculated to save the parent's face during the years that such control can legally be exercised, whereas when the child is finally in a position to defy such control the parent can only regard him as one among other adults—free to steer his own course . . . .

There is, however, a second kind of authority by constraint which is more commonly used than that of physical force, and which is more subtle in its effects on the child. This is what is often described by parents as ruling by love. Here the intention is by appeals to the child's affection to bring his action into line with the parent's wishes. This seems to us the Unpardonable Sin in the sphere of family relationships. It does violence to the child's free feeling of love for the parent by turning it to some ulterior purpose.

William E. Blatz and Helen Bott
THE MANAGEMENT OF YOUNG CHILDREN

Some days, try writing about a part of your life as if it were a movie or a play. Describe the scene as someone outside would see it—the viewer or audience. Step outside yourself and try to describe what you do and say as if you were one of the characters in the performance.

. . . and though she feels as if she's in a play, she is anyway . . .

John Lennon and Paul McCartney
"PENNY LANE"

What kind of person do you dislike?

Sit among a group of people. Watch them. What are they doing with their time? Would you say any of them were wasting time or fooling around? Before you answer that, you should define for yourself what it means to "waste time" or "fool around."

122

"If it were up to me, I'd . . ."

In the pages of your journal, it can be up to you. What changes would you make?

together."

Ahead was a mounted policeman in
khaki ⭐ directing traffic. The car
slowed suddenly pressing Duff closer
against me.
"Yes," I said. "It's nice as hell
to think so."

The End.

Paris-Sept. 21-1925

"Isn't it nice to think so"

Last page of notebook draft of *The Sun Also Rises*, with Brett (Ashley) appearing as Duff (Twysden), her real name. Passage incomplete; neither version of last line final.

Trouble in the park last night. More and more kids have been gathering there throughout the summer and since school started even more. People from the big houses complaining more and more. Big white houses. Wide lawns. Fences. Hedges. Two station wagons. Sometimes shouting from their lawns. There have been letters to the editor. But no one tried to clear the park. What goes on in the park: talking, eating, radios, drinking, some drugs, some sex. But no real trouble. Okay, there are some people who shouldn't be there, and things happen there that shouldn't. But not much. Much more talking, laughing, walking than anything else. But the letters and complaints are all about drinking, drugs, sex. Last night the cops clear the park. Shouting back and forth, cops and kids. Kids shout and taunt, then run in a group to another spot, shout and taunt, then run again. Hit and run. Here, my home town. I'm caught in it. I'm afraid and I'm excited and I'm proud and I'm ashamed. Afraid of being hurt. Afraid of being caught. Excited by excitement. Excited by everyone running and shouting. Proud of our kids' strength. Ashamed of the mess we're making. What will happen next—tomorrow and after that?

Terry Phelps
JOURNAL

People with small minds talk about other people; people with average minds talk about events; people with great minds talk about ideas.

Write a speech attacking something or someone.

∴ : :

A WORD HAS POWER IN AND OF ITSELF. IT COMES FROM NOTHING INTO SOUND AND MEANING; IT GIVES ORIGIN TO ALL THINGS. BY MEANS OF WORDS CAN A MAN DEAL WITH THE WORLD ON EQUAL TERMS. AND THE WORD IS SACRED. A MAN'S NAME IS HIS OWN; HE CAN KEEP IT OR GIVE IT AWAY AS HE LIKES. UNTIL RECENT TIMES, THE KIOWAS WOULD NOT SPEAK THE NAME OF A DEAD MAN. TO DO SO WOULD HAVE BEEN DISRESPECTFUL AND DISHONEST. THE DEAD TAKE THEIR NAMES WITH THEM OUT OF THE WORLD.

N. Scott Momaday
THE WAY TO RAINY MOUNTAIN

In California the schools I attended were all Anglo except for this little mexicanito. At least, I never knew anyone who admitted he was Mexican and I certainly never thought to ask. When my name was accented incorrectly, Réndon instead of Rendón, that was all right; finally I must have gotten tired of correcting people or just didn't bother.

Armando B. Rendon
CHICANO MANIFESTO

Give a different answer to each of the following questions.
Who are you?
Who are you?
Who are you?
Who are you?
Who are you?
Who are you?
Who are you?
Who are you?
Who are you?
Who are you?

Try to write about the places you know as if you were traveling and seeing them for the first time. What are some of the features of the scenery? What are the local people like? Do you see any unusual characters? What impression does the place make on you as an outside observer?

I voyage through the toilet-tiled halls
into my empty study; empty though the walls
hang fat with books. I look about me
aimlessly, thumb through dumb anthologies
from Beowulf to James Baldwin: I'm caught by Lovelace—
"Stone walls do not a prison make,
Nor iron bars a cage—"
I see dirty windows and dull red brick;
my subjective correlatives become cheap tricks. Shipwrecked
in my armchair, I sip a vodka on the rocks.

Irving Weinman

Once when I was little my grandmother took me to a funeral parlor. I'm not sure whether one of her friends died or if it was some relative that I don't remember. I'm not even sure how old I was. But I remember the place, and I remember the lady in the coffin. She was really thin, and she was wearing a blue dress that was shiny, like satin. She had pearls, or some other kind of necklace, around her neck. My grandmother took me with her up to the coffin—she didn't look at the woman much, but I did, and while we were standing there a fly came in and settled on the woman's face. And while I watched, the fly walked around on her face. I must have known how odd that was—it meant that the woman was completely dead—no, that's stupid, when you're dead you're dead. But anyone alive would twitch or brush the fly away—it doesn't seem human to be so still. The woman didn't seem human anymore. Maybe you could say she wasn't. Anyway, I see that woman whenever I think of somebody dying—and sometimes I dream about her.

Gail Phinney
JOURNAL

Moods. Individuals have them. Groups have them. Whole nations seem to have them. They are never stable. What are yours like? What seems to bring them on? What are your recurring moods? What mood are you in now? Can you describe it? Not in general terms, but can you instead describe *exactly* how you feel?

Cemetery of El Kettar. An overcast sky and a heavy sea facing hills covered with white tombstones. The trees and earth damp from the rain. Pigeons among the white ledger stones. One solitary geranium, its leaves both pink and red, and a great silent feeling of loss and sadness that teaches us to know the pure and beautiful face of death.

Albert Camus
NOTEBOOKS, 1935-1942

Make a list of books you never want to read again, places you never want to go again, people you hope you'll never see again, or things you hope you'll never have to do again.

Pick two things that are important to you, two things that seem very dissimilar. Try to discover whether they have some quality in common that reveals something about you.

The Black Sheep

In a far-off country many years ago there lived a Black Sheep. They shot him.

A century later, the repentant flock erected an equestrian statue of him, which looked very good in the park.

From then on, every time Black Sheep appeared they were promptly executed so that future generations of common, ordinary sheep could also indulge in sculpture.

Augusto Monterroso
THE BLACK SHEEP AND OTHER FABLES

While listening to a conversation between two people, write as much as you can of what they are saying. Unless you know and can rapidly take some sort of shorthand, you will probably not be able to get down every word. How will you decide what to write?

"You'll drive yourself crazy caring about everything," he said. "You just can't."

"But I do. . . ."

"Look, take me," Andrez continued. "*I* don't care. You're going to drive yourself insane. Me—? I just clown around. I'm apathetic." Underneath the humor of his explanation there was bitterness. I felt I was seeing through the mask he wore every day in school. He was revealing to me in a moment of honesty why he joked and bounced from table to table in the lunchroom. He couldn't afford to care. He wouldn't survive if he allowed himself to be like me. He was playing a role out of necessity.

I respected him much more after our conversation. Within a matter of forty minutes we opened ourselves to one another and exposed our inner feelings. We came to understand what made the other react as he did. For Andrez this was a rare happening and I admired him for lifting his facade and showing himself.

Susan Gregory
HEY, WHITE GIRL

One evening a professor of logic was out walking his dog. When in the course of his perambulation he passed the college library, his attention was directed to a man's call for help from one of the windows in the building.

"What's your trouble?" called out the kindly professor.

"I got locked in here by mistake," was the response. "Get the janitor to open the door and let me out."

The professor of logic stopped to think about it for a few seconds, then replied: "No person can be in the library after 6 P. M. You are a person. Therefore you are not in the library." Whereupon he resumed his walk.

Ralph L. Woods
HOW TO TORTURE YOUR MIND

A thing cannot have a property unless it is there to have it, and since unicorns . . . *do* have the property of being thought of, there certainly must be such things. When I think of a unicorn, what I am thinking of is certainly not nothing; if it were nothing, then, when I think of a griffin, I should also be thinking of nothing and there would be no difference between thinking of a griffin and thinking of a unicorn. But there certainly is a difference; and what can the difference be except that in one case what I am thinking of is a unicorn, and in the other a griffin? And if the unicorn is what I am thinking of, then there certainly must *be* a unicorn, in spite of the fact that unicorns are unreal. In other words, though in one sense of the words there certainly *are* no unicorns—that sense, namely, in which to assert that there are would be equivalent to asserting that unicorns are real—yet there must be some other sense in which there *are* such things, since, if there were not, we could not think of them.

G. E. Moore
PHILOSOPHICAL STUDIES

Wilbur Glenn Voliva, of Zion, Illinois, made several trips around the world and at the end of each announced that the earth was "as flat as a pancake." In addition to predicting the end of the world for 1923, 1927, 1930, 1935, and 1943, Mr. Voliva stated that the wearing of a hat is necessary to thinking because the headpiece holds the brains in balance.

And Mr. Voliva was confident he had routed the scientists when he asked: "Where is the man who believes he can jump into the air, remaining off the earth one second, and come down to earth 193.7 miles from where he jumped up?"

Ralph L. Woods

Describe an event that you witnessed as a detached, disinterested observer. How might your account differ from one written by a participant in the event?

annalist n. a person who keeps a written record of yearly events.
annals n.pl. (L *annalis* from *annus* year) 1. written account of events year by year in chronological order. 2. historical records or chronicles; history. 3. *sing.* the record of a single year of events.

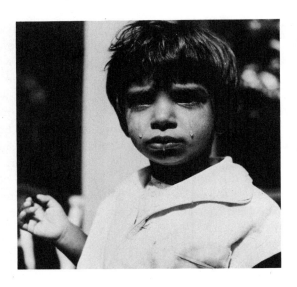

Try looking back at something you've already written in your journal. Consider it a beginning. Probe deeper and add to it. Try to add details that you may have overlooked the first time around. Or write this time about your feelings and reactions about what you had written earlier.

Look for colors in the world around you—sometimes they will turn up in surprising places. For practice, try to find an object to match each of the following colors: white, gray, red, scarlet, crimson, pink, rose, vermillion, yellow, gold, orange, blue, azure, green, violet, purple, brown, and black.

Describe a busy bustling scene, such as a department store just before Christmas. Repeat, describing a quiet scene.

There is a cardinal rule of travel, all too often overlooked, that I call *The Law of Inverse Appreciation.*

It states: "The less there is between you and the environment, the more you appreciate that environment."

Colin Fletcher

Choose an outdoor scene and describe it during each of the seasons. Consider it from the same point of view each time and be careful to point out the similarities as well as the differences from one season to the next.

Ticklish Question

Have you ever tried to tickle yourself? You cannot. Darwin suggested that "the precise point to be touched must not be known" if a tickle is really to tickle. However, several investigators in England reported that _____

_____

The solitary soldier stood
erect
disdaining reason's
awesome army arrayed against him.

Cold guns spat
frozen bullets
at his bare breast.
Howitzers hurled their heavy charges
through the crackling air.
Tanks trundled across the tundra field
their shrill cannons shuddering.
And gelid bombs
split
the glacial ground.

Strong and sound he stood
suffering
not
this fearsome fusillade.

The chill smoke slowly cleared.
Reason's ragged remnants
their force spent
ignored
blasphemed
in shabby silhouette
departed.

Steadfast still he stood,
surveyed
the icy aftermath
of war's wintry wasteland,
and then

turned.

A touch
as gentle as a downy breast
caressed
his stiffness.
Purple heat
pulsed through his awakening form.

Fragile trying to be strong
no more,
he slumped
sagged
sank to the earth
in

ultimate surrender.

Greta Rose
JOURNAL

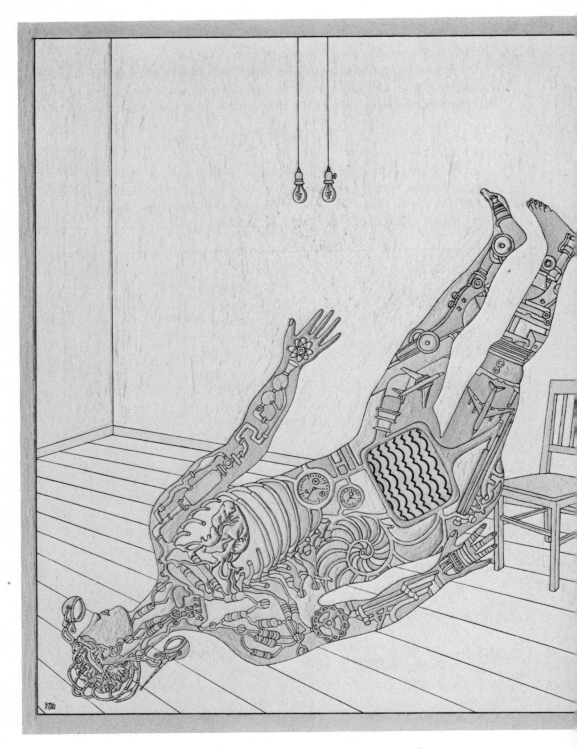

I hear ... and I forget
I see ... and I remember
I do ... and I understand
                    Chinese proverb

Try to remember all you can of a particular event that occurred when you were much younger. Keep focused on this one event and avoid distraction. Take notes on the details that you remember; look at these notes after a few days have passed to see if you can add to them.

Today I got up at six-thirty and put on my uniform. My dad gave me a ride to the hospital and I reported on time. Dan came a few moments later and we waited around until Miss Morrisey showed up and we went to work. I had three patients to take care of in the morning. I fed, washed, and reclothed the patients and got them into wheelchairs. Then I made their beds. I washed my hands about twice as much as yesterday. Mr. Loomis spit in my hand and a real sexy girl asked me to help her dress (which I reluctantly declined) and I got a nurse. Dan and I fooled around and insulted each other all through breaks. Mr. Young is weird. He broke both of his legs and all he does is tell me what to do about everything. He insults people and winks at every girl, even Miss Morrisey, and calls everyone cutie. He asked me, "Hey, kid, why are you so fat?" It was an average day and on the whole a good one.

George Keen
JOURNAL

Consider an assortment of objects, such as you might find in your desk drawer. Categorize them according to size, physical characteristics, and any other aspects you think appropriate.

souvenir n. (F *souvenir,* to remember) something kept and serving as a reminder of a place, an occasion, or a person; keepsake; memento.

Don't overlook the possibility of using your journal to collect things that other people say or write that you find especially interesting.

I was still sitting on the porch when they got back. My first thought was that they didn't go all the way to Woodville, they were back so quick, but I could tell that they had gotten married. When Raymond parked the car, I could hear the radio blaring rock-and-roll. Mama was grinning down. For the first time in a couple of weeks they were talking to each other. Raymond got out of the car, leaving the radio on, and went on down toward the hog pen, looking as if it was slowly dawning on him that he had just gotten married. Mama remained in the car listening to the song on the radio. All of a sudden she got out of the car and started twisting to the fast beat. Her big pregnant belly swayed from side to side.

Anne Moody
COMING OF AGE IN MISSISSIPPI

It has been said that no art can capture our total experience of an instant of time. Something is missing from every record. While writing is strong in recording thoughts and sequences, it is weak in its ability to capture *simultaneity*—the experience of several things through several senses at once. Some modern writers experiment with ways to stretch writing beyond what have seemed to be its limits and try to capture simultaneous occurrences. They abandon the straight-line, one-word-after-another arrangement of writing and spill words across a page so that they have some of the instant impact of a photograph or painting but still have the thought and meaning of words and writing. Experiment with unconventional ways to capture the total experience of an instant of your life.

From the beginning I had trouble getting into the helmet. The procedure was to stick the thumbs in the helmet's earholes and stretch the helmet out as it came down over the head, a matter of lateral pull, easy enough if you practiced isometrics, but I never had the strength to get my ears quite clear, so they were bent double inside the helmet once it was on. I would work a finger up inside to get the ears upright again, a painful procedure and noisy, the sounds sharp in the confines of the hard shell of the helmet as I twisted and murmured, until it was done, the ears ringing softly, quiet then in the helmet, secure as being in a turret. Then I would look out beyond the bars of the nose guard—the "cage" the players call it—to see what was going on outside, my eyes still watering slightly. It was more difficult to get the helmet off.

George Plimpton
PAPER LION

134

Write about your day as if you were writing a news story.

A REMARKABLE INVENTION!

DR. SCOTT'S

ELECTRIC

NO MATCHES REQUIRED.

The finest Cigarette ever made. **Turkish Tobacco and Rice Paper.** They never fail to light without matches in the strongest gale, and for the Theatre, Cab, Carriage, Yachting, Fishing, Hunting, on the Ocean and for home, office, and street use, they will be found **Exceedingly Convenient. No Nicotine** can be taken into the system while smoking these Cigarettes, as in the mouth-piece of each is placed a small wad of absorbent cotton, which strains and

CIGARETTES

LIGHT ON THE BOX.

eliminates the injurious qualities from the smoke. **Give them one trial.** Price, 10 cents per box of 10. If you cannot get them at your cigar store, hotel, or druggist's, remit us 25 cents, 50 cents, or $1, and we will **mail boxes** containing 20, 50, or 100 Cigarettes, postpaid. If not entirely satisfactory, we will return the money.

Address :

SCOTT & CHAMBERLIN,

842 BROADWAY, N.Y.

BEWARE OF CHEAP CIGARETTES!

☞ It is a matter of regret that many manufacturers of Tobacco and Cigarettes, devoid of all conscience, are now flooding the market with goods of a most injurious quality. DR. SCOTT'S are guaranteed pure and harmless. $1000 will be paid in every case where it is proven that these Cigarettes are adulterated or contain anything but Pure Tobacco. WE CHALLENGE ANALYSIS. Mention this paper.

RELIABLE AGENTS WANTED IN EVERY TOWN.

July 19—My cousin Ricky came to visit last weekend and got on everyone's nerves as soon as he stepped out of the car. I can't spend more than a few minutes with that kid. He gets at everybody—if he's not pestering, he's whining—if he's not whining, he's breaking something. Most people wouldn't mind the sort of thing he does if it came from a child of six or seven—they could excuse it because of his age, but from a kid of eleven it's too much to take. This time he did himself in. He was fooling around with the exhaust for the circulating pump down at the pool, pressing his stomach up against the grate over the opening—that leaves little marks because of the suction—little red circles. The last time he did it, the pump must have switched into high, and he got stuck to the grate. He couldn't pull himself off and started screaming. Two of us had to run over to pull him off, and when we did, his skin was purple and bruised in the pattern of the grate. I knew it was painful, and all the adults did too, but I think all of us took some pleasure in seeing him caught by his own stupidity.

Joyce Rodgerson
JOURNAL

What situations make you nervous? While different situations affect people in different ways, certain ones, such as sitting in a dentist's waiting room or taking a test in school, make many people nervous.

Citizen Pollution Report

To report a pollution problem or emergency, be sure to obtain the basic information a water pollution official will require in order to take prompt action.

Copies of the report should be sent to your local and state water pollution control agency as soon as possible. The following details should be included in the report:

1. Location—name of stream, lake or water and exact place (by reference to identifiable land marks).
2. Date and time observed.
3. Nature of pollutant—oil, scum, algae, foam, garbage, raw sewage, floating debris, etc.
4. Appearance: color, odor—describe.

5. Fish or wildlife affected: fish, frogs, turtles, waterfowl, birds or other species—estimate numbers.
6. Source of pollution, if found, industrial or municipal outfall, septic tank outlet, drain tile, manure lagoon or other lagoon overflow, oil rig, commercial vessel, marina, etc.
7. Name and address of alleged polluter.
8. Your own name, address and phone number and the same information for other known witnesses.

Izaak Walton League of America

Self-Portrait by Oskar Kokoschka. 1913.

Collection, The Museum of Modern Art, New York.

At nineteen I was a stranger to myself. At forty I asked: who am I? At fifty I concluded I would never know.

Know thyself is a wise Socratic exhortation, but how is it possible? Do I even understand a tithe of my nature. In truth, I know nothing about anybody, least of all about myself. No matter what I do it is likely to be wrong; one bungles everything, for the brain is feeble and intuition is a saline and marshy guess. Whatever one is done he will do; that is his character, and he can neither improve nor escape it.

Who is wise, except by accident? When I am intelligent I am startled; should I be as melancholy as Avernus I am baffled. Making ready for an agreeable conversation with a friend, a seizure of unsuspected spleen overtakes me. Then there are strokes of idiocy and the unreasonable gales of mirth. Who can fathom these blowsy hours of vacancy, or say unto himself: this moment I propose to be meditative? As for my paltry virtues, there is no looking glass in which I can observe them.

Now sunset writes for me, and rain scribbles my woe. I cannot level my life. I walk upon my hurts which readers entitle my books; what else, then, can this memoir be but an enchiridion of my chagrins and shames?

                    Edward Dahlberg

I study myself microscopically. I put my finger on the exact place of the fault, the unadmitted sliding. For the mind is more reptilian than even you, Gentlemen. It slips away like snakes, it slips away until it affects our tongues, I mean it leaves them hanging.

I am the man who has best charted his inmost self, his most imperceptible slitherings. Really, I lose myself in my thought the way one dreams, the way one suddenly returns to his thought. I am the man who knows the innermost recesses of loss.

Antonin Artaud
"HERE IS SOMEONE . . ."

Make it thy business to know thyself, which is the most difficult lesson in the world.

Cervantes
DON QUIXOTE

"Why then do you mortal men seek after happiness outside yourselves, when it lies within you? You are led astray by error and ignorance. I will briefly show you what complete happiness hinges upon. If I ask you whether there is anything more precious to you than your own self, you will say no. So if you are in possession of yourself you will possess something you would never wish to lose and something Fortune could never take away."

Boethius

One can bring no greater reproach against a man than to say that he does not set sufficient value upon pleasure, and there is no greater sign of a fool than the thinking that he can tell at once and easily what it is that pleases him. To know this is not easy, and to extend our knowledge of it is the highest and most neglected of all arts and branches of education. Indeed, if we could solve the difficulty of knowing what gives us pleasure, if we could find its springs, its inception and earliest *modus operandi,* we should have discovered the secret of life and development.

Samuel Butler
NOTE-BOOKS

139

A Discovery of Old Age

Perhaps the best is always cumulative. One's eating and drinking one wants fresh, and for the nonce, right off, and have done with it—but I would not give a straw for that person or poem, or friend, or city, or work of art, that was not more grateful the second time than the first—and more still the third. Nay, I do not believe any grandest eligibility ever comes forth at first. In my own experience, (persons, poems, places, characters,) I discover the best hardly ever at first, (no absolute rule about it, however,) sometimes suddenly bursting forth, or stealthily opening to me, perhaps after years of unwitting familiarity, unappreciation, usage.

Walt Whitman

Wednesday, November 7th

And this shall be written for my own pleasure. But that phrase inhibits me; for if one writes only for one's own pleasure, I don't know what it is that happens. I suppose the convention of writing is destroyed: therefore one does not write at all.

A WRITER'S DIARY
BEING EXTRACTS FROM THE DIARY OF VIRGINIA WOOLF

Is it safe to walk down your street at night, or does that scare the daylights out of you?

One Day of Crime in Washington, D.C.

Friday, December 9, 1966:
9:15 A.M.   Strongarm robbery, street, $2.
10:00 A.M. Armed robbery, liquor store, $1,500.
11:30 A.M. Pocketbook snatched with force and violence, street, $3.
12:30 P.M. Holdup with revolver, roofing company, $2,100.
2:40 P.M.   Holdup with gun, shoe store, $139.
3:20 P.M.   Holdup with gun, apartment, $92.
4:55 P.M.   Holdup with gun, bank, $8,716.
6:25 P.M.   Mugging, street, $5.
6:50 P.M.   Holdup with revolver, tourist home, $30.
7:00 P.M.   Strongarm robbery, street, $25.
7:05 P.M.   Holdup with gun, auto in parking lot, $61.
7:10 P.M.   Strongarm robbery, apartment house, $3.
7:15 P.M.   Holdup with revolver (employee shot twice), truck rental company, $200.
7:25 P.M.   Mugging, street, $5.
7:50 P.M.   Holdup with gun, transfer company, $1,400.
8:55 P.M.   Holdup with shotgun, newspaper substation, $100.
10:10 P.M. Holdup with gun, hotel, $289.50.
10:15 P.M. Strongarm robbery, street, $120.
10:30 P.M. Holdup with gun, street, $59.50.
10:53 P.M. Strongarm robbery, street, $175.
11:05 P.M. Holdup, tavern, $40.
11:30 P.M. Strongarm robbery, street, $3.
11:55 P.M. Strongarm robbery, street, $51.

Saturday, December 10:
12:20 A.M. Strongarm robbery, street, $19.
1:10 A.M.   Strongarm robbery, apartment house, $3.
3:25 A.M.   Strongarm robbery, street, $25.
3:50 A.M.   Holdup with knife, street, $23.
3:55 A.M.   Holdup with gun, street, $25.
4:20 A.M.   Robbery with intent to rape, street, 75 cents.
4:20 A.M.   Holdup with gun, carryout shop, $80.
6:25 A.M.   Holdup-rape, street, $20.
6:25 A.M.   Holdup with gun, tourist home, no amount listed.
6:45 A.M.   Holdup, street, $5.
7:30 A.M.   Holdup with knife, cleaners, $300.
7:40 A.M.   Strongarm robbery, street, $80.

For a few days, follow in a newspaper some issue that interests you, angers you, amuses you, or otherwise arouses a strong reaction in you. Use your journal as a soap-box to pour out your ideas, opinions, and emotions on the issue.

. . . Kay knew of what she was afraid: it was a memory, a childish memory of terrors that once, long ago, had hovered above her like haunted limbs on a tree of night. Aunts, cooks, strangers—each eager to spin a tale or teach a rhyme of spooks and death, omens, spirits, demons. And always there had been the unfailing threat of the wizard man: stay close to the house, child, else a wizard man'll snatch you and eat you alive! He lived everywhere, the wizard man, and everywhere was danger. At night, in bed, hear him rapping at the window? Listen!

Truman Capote

A house is never still in darkness to those who listen intently; there is a whispering in distant chambers, an unearthly hand presses the snib of the window, the latch rises. Ghosts were created when the first man awoke in the night.

J. M. Barrie

I was pretty tired, and the first thing I knowed I was asleep. When I woke up I didn't know where I was for a minute. I set up and looked around, a little scared. Then I remembered. The river looked miles and miles across. The moon was so bright I could a counted the drift logs that went a slipping along, black and still, hundreds of yards out from shore. Everything was dead quiet, and it looked late, and smelt late. You know what I mean—I don't know the words to put it in.

Mark Twain
HUCK FINN

142

Night - a damp chill penetrates this small room, the rain smudges and softens the lights from the flickering signs outside, and the wind pushes sheets of water along the shiny pavement and against the scarred stucco walls of this prison, my house. The door rattles like a shivering skeleton. The single bare bulb hanging by a frayed cord swings slowly back and forth throwing its harsh light on the lunar landscape of the ceiling. The heavy iron radiator under the window sill has been turned off and stands like a rib cage removed from a prehistoric mammal frozen for eons in the arctic ice cap. It is cold to the touch, a leaden liquid coldness that flows to the very marrow of the bones.

I want to get out - away from this dungeon, but I am a prisoner here. Why do I say that? There are no bars on my window, no locks on my door. I'm free to go, free to walk out of this chilly, cold, confining room, free to run into the drenching abyss of this dark night. But something stops me. I don't know what. Are the bars on my heart? The lock on my mind?

Hank Spivak
Journal

At night when people
No longer stir,
That's when I come alive.
My heart can start to beat again.
There is no need for me
To turn my face
From people.
I seem to breathe with ease.

Sharon Damon
JOURNAL

Bernard Peache testify'd, That being in Bed on a Lords-day Night, he heard a scrabbling at the Window, whereat he then saw Susanna Martin come in, and jump down upon the Floor. She took hold of this Deponents Feet, and drawing his Body up into an Heap, she lay upon him near Two Hours; in all which time he could neither speak nor stirr. At length, when he could begin to move, he laid hold on her Hand, and pulling it up to his mouth, he bit three of her Fingers, as he judged, unto the Bone. Whereupon she went from the Chamber, down the Stairs, out at the Door. This Deponent thereupon called unto the people of the House, to advise them of what passed; and he himself did follow her. The people saw her not; but there being a Bucket at the Left-hand of the Door, there was a drop of Blood found on it; and several more drops of Blood upon the Snow newly fallen abroad. There was likewise the print of her two Feet just without the Threshold; but no more sign of any Footing further off.

Cotton Mather
THE TRIAL OF SUSANNA MARTIN

"Do all of you sleep on this one mattress?"

"That ain't nothin', brother. There's a poor fella livin' down the hall what's got six children and their place ain't no bigger'n this. There was eight of 'em till two of the younguns got drafted in the army a month or so ago."

"Where's your toilet and bathroom?"

"Take him down the hall and show him, Lil. Show him good." Lil, his wife, nodded toward me and I followed her down a dark corridor, where she opened a door and pointed in. There was an old bathtub with most of the enamel broken off and a filthy toilet. The seat next to it had rotted and fallen apart, lying in a heap of other decaying boards and fallen plaster. The foul air was unbearable. "Would you wash your child in that mess?" she asked. I didn't answer. I knew she didn't expect me to. I just took a picture of it; and we went back to her husband and children.

"Well, how'd you like it? It's a dog, huh?" I nodded, and he went on, "Eight families use it, brother. See that baseball bat over there in the corner? Well, my boy there don't play ball with it. We kill rats with it."

Gordon Parks

144

All that we see or seem
Is but a dream within a dream

Edgar Allen Poe

When we are sleeping naturally, it is not necessary to believe, as has often been supposed, that our senses are closed to external sensations. Our senses continue to be active. They act, it is true, with less precision, but in compensation they embrace a host of "subjective" impressions which pass unperceived when we are awake — for then we live in a world of perceptions common to all men — and which reappear in sleep, when we live only for ourselves. Thus our faculty of sense perception, far from being narrowed during sleep at all points, is on the contrary extended, at least in certain directions, in its field of operations.

Henri Bergson

The Day

The day was a year at first
When children ran in the garden;
The day shrank down to a month
When the boys played ball.

The day was a week thereafter
When young men walked in the garden;
The day was itself a day
When love grew tall.

The day shrank down to an hour
When old men limped in the garden;
The day will last forever
When it is nothing at all.

Theodore Spencer

See the minutes, how they run,
How many make the hour full complete;
How many hours bring about the day;
How many days will finish up the year;
How many years a mortal man may live.

Shakespeare

Meeting a Hermit

I found in one of my rambles up the hills a real hermit, living in a lonesome spot, hard to get at, rocky, the view fine, with a little patch of land two rods square. A man of youngish middle age, city born and raised, had been to school, had travel'd in Europe and California. I first met him once or twice on the road, and pass'd the time of day, with some small talk; then, the third time, he ask'd me to go along a bit and rest in his hut (an almost unprecedented compliment, as I heard from others afterwards.) He was of Quaker stock, I think; talk'd with ease and moderate freedom, but did not unbosom his life, or story, or tragedy, or whatever it was.

Walt Whitman
AUTOBIOGRAPHIA OR THE STORY OF A LIFE

from *The Herblock Gallery*
(Simon & Schuster, 1968)

February 7, 1878. —For two hours I have been idly wandering around the woods and pond, lugging my chair, picking out choice spots to sit awhile—then up and slowly on again. All is peace here. Of course, none of the summer noises or vitality: to-day hardly even winter ones. I amuse myself by exercising my voice in recitations, and in ringing the changes on all the vocal and alphabetical sounds. Not even an echo; only the cawing of a solitary crow, flying at some distance.

Walt Whitman
AUTOBIOGRAPHIA OR THE STORY OF A LIFE

38   *ECLECTIC SERIES.*

LESSON XVI.

fụll	lōad	hĕav'y	mĭd'dle	hĕav'i er
slĭp	wrŏng	hănd'le	brŏth'er	de çēived'

A KIND BROTHER.

1. A boy was once sent from home to take a basket of things to his grandmother.

2. The basket was so full that it was very heavy. So his little brother went with him, to help carry the load.

SECOND READER.   39

3. They put a pole under the handle of the basket, and each then took hold of an end of the pole. In this way they could carry the basket very nicely.

4. Now the older boy thought, "My brother Tom does not know about this pole.

5. "If I slip the basket near him, his side will be heavy, and mine light; but if the basket is in the middle of the pole, it will be as heavy for me as it is for him.

6. "Tom does not know this as I do. But I will not do it. It would be wrong, and I will not do what is wrong."

7. Then he slipped the basket quite near his own end of the pole. His load was now heavier than that of his little brother.

8. Yet he was happy; for he felt that he had done right. Had he deceived his brother, he would not have felt at all happy.

Describe a favor that someone did for you. Why did he do it? How did you feel? What did you do?

Use your journal to criticize—people, their actions, events, ideas, films, music, books, ... A critic evaluates something according to the standards he has established for himself. The best critics try first to understand something on its own terms, measuring it against its own standards before they measure it against their own. What *are* your standards? Where do they come from?

What bothered me about my step-mother? Everything. I just don't like her because she didn't like me. Everything I did was always wrong . . . I couldn't do nothing right no matter what I did. You'd just walk out the back door and she'd say that you closed it the wrong way. It seemed like everything I did was always wrong, no matter what I did. My dad was, you might say, an aggressive guy and around him about everything I did was about the same way . . . it was wrong too.

THE UNEMPLOYED: A SOCIAL-PSYCHOLOGICAL PORTRAIT

I remember Bunny Van Valkenburg's father Doc. He was our family doctor. I remember him telling of a patient he had who got poison ivy inside his body. The man was in total misery but it healed very fast because there was no way that he could scratch it.

I remember not being able to pronounce "mirror."

I remember an ice cream parlor in Tulsa that had a thing called a pig's dinner. It was like a very big banana split in a wooden dish made like a pig's trough. If you ate it all they gave you a certificate saying that you ate it all.

I remember a spooky job I had once cleaning up a dentist's office after everyone had gone home. I had my own key. The only part I liked was straightening up the magazines in the waiting room. I saved it as the last thing to do.

Joe Brainard
from "I REMEMBER"

It is a strange experience reading your diary forty or fifty years after you've written it. I began mine while I was still an undergraduate in 1915. I have kept it up ever since. I don't know what first impelled me to start it—perhaps an unconscious impulse to salvage each day from oblivion. . . . Reading this diary—sixty volumes . . . is very different from reading history; there the characters are all strangers and dead. Here, they are alive and present. Characters keep appearing whose very existence I had forgotten, and yet they keep reappearing, vivid ghosts, taut in their momentary preoccupations, clamped, as I myself was, in the imperatives of NOW. Reading through these pages, I can foresee their destinies; their futures are laid out, all the crisscrossed lines where my life

149

intersected theirs. It is somewhat terrible to become possessed, suddenly, of all that foresight . . . . They seem blindfolded, as I myself was.

S. N. Behrman
PEOPLE IN A DIARY

those who cannot remember the past   are condemned to repeat it

george santayana, the life of reason,

Freedom

Freedom is not following a river.
Freedom is following a river,
  though, if you want to.
It is deciding now by what happens now.
It is knowing that luck makes a difference.

No leader is free; no follower is free—
  the rest of us can often be free.
Most of the world are living by
  creeds too odd, chancey, and habit-forming
  to be worth arguing about by reason.

If you are oppressed, wake up about
  four in the morning: most places,
  you can usually be free some of the time
  if you wake up before other people.

                                    William Stafford

. . . Like the utopians who preceded him, Skinner hopes for a
society in which men of good will can work, love and live in security and
harmony. For mankind he wants enough to eat, a clean environment, and
safety from nuclear cataclysm. He longs for a world-wide culture based on
the principles of his famous didactic novel, *Walden Two.* Those principles
include: communal ownership of land and buildings, egalitarian
relationships between men and women, devotion to art, music and
literature, liberal rewards for constructive behavior, freedom from
jealousy, gossip, and—astonishingly—from the ideal of freedom . . . .
. . . we can no longer afford freedom, and so it must be replaced
with control over man, his conduct and his culture. . . .

                                                              TIME

151

Freedom

Here I am, speeding down the highway.
Going fast, faster, faster.
Going far, farther, farther away from
Problems, troubles.
Finally, here it is:
Freedom at last. . . .

Marty Bushee
JOURNAL

FREEDOM
IS JUST ANOTHER WORD
FOR NOTHING LEFT TO LOSE.

Kris Kristofferson

The TV image of the black man is enormously superior to that of the white person—especially on color TV. This is also true of the Oriental and of the American Indian.

It is simply due to the fact that the TV image is itself iconic. It favors the contour, the mask, the sculptured form. The play of light and shade in the white countenance, to say nothing of the habitual effort at individual facial expression, renders the white person hopelessly inferior on the TV medium.

Marshall McLuhan
CULTURE IS OUR BUSINESS
[adapted slightly]

152

One of the most compelling features of Japanese Haiku poetry is its capacity to provide in a few brief lines an image of almost universal proportions. In the lines

> *Now my loneliness*
> *After the fireworks*
> *Look, a falling star*

the reader finds himself in a moment of interrupted solitude and, at the same time, perceives that the contrast between excitement and isolation is common to all men. What would his reaction be, however, if the poet had added color to certain words of the poem! Would the thoughts and feelings about the experience or the broader implications of the poem be any different if the words *loneliness, fireworks,* or *star* appeared in pink as opposed to deep blue? A number of recent experiments have shown that the coloration of words has a powerful impact on one's feelings about and interpretation of poetry. Light shades produce different reactions than dark shades, and blues elicit different associations than reds, although the words and form of the poem remain unchanged.

If colors have such a substantial impact when associated with the written word, is it not also possible that the pigmentation of skin may affect a person's feelings about other people and his interpretation of their actions? In particular, is it possible that color differences may play a divisive role in social relationships? The question is an intriguing one inasmuch as the major work on race prejudice and social conflict has used color simply as a way of designating the battle lines. Much less attention has been paid to the possibility that color may be partially responsible for the battle itself.

John Hope Franklin
COLOR AND RACE

Success is counted sweetest
By those who ne'er succeed.
EMILY DICKINSON

153

THIS CAN BE YOUR "BIG BREAK"
if you're a man who doesn't want to be...

Write about something that you wanted very much—and maybe worked long and hard for—but were not able to get.

There is no technical reason why someone like Sears Roebuck should not come out tomorrow with an appliance selling for less than a TV set, capable of being plugged in wherever there is electricity, and giving immediate access to all the information needed for schoolwork from first grade through college.

Peter F. Drucker

What would you like: Education by injection? A catalog of spare body parts? A larger, more efficient brain? A cure for old age? Immortality through freezing? Parentless children? Custom-ordered body size and skin color? The ability to convert sunlight directly into energy, just as plants do, without utilizing food as an intermediary? Name it, and somebody is seriously proposing it.

Albert Rosenfeld

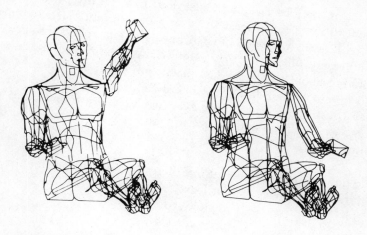

Four Types of Modern Man

1. The Healthy Man: "Two plus two equals four. Isn't that interesting?"
2. The Neurotic: "Two plus two equals four, but I can't *stand* it."
3. The Psychotic: "Two plus two equals five."
4. The Valueless Man: "Two plus two equals four. So what?"

Much Madness is divinest Sense—
To a discerning Eye—
Much Sense—the starkest Madness—

In this, as All, prevail—
Assent—and you are sane—
Demur—you're straightway dangerous—
And handled with a Chain—

Emily Dickinson

I had so many jobs I just can't remember many of them. . . only those in the last three or four years. I've probably had about 150 jobs in my life . . . some of them I didn't like and only worked there a couple of hours and just walked out. I've lived and traveled around the whole country . . . I've been just about everywhere in the last seven or eight years. Most of the jobs I've had I just quit them on my own.

I went to work for at least three or four different plastic companies and worked less than a week in each one. Two of those I was sent by the state employment office . . . they referred me there, and the other a friend told me about. After the last plastic job it got cold where I was in Maine so I went to Florida and I worked as a bus boy in a hotel down there. My cousin goes down there ever' winter and a friend has a job down there as a bellhop and he got the job for me . . . talked to the boss and got me hired. . . .

I've done just about everything there is to do at one time or another. . . . I think I must have had at least 150 jobs.

— Unemployed
Thirty years old
High School Graduate
Single
Caucasian

The main thing that is troubling me right now, at the present time, is future developments . . . I mean, am I going to be able to develop into something . . . am I going to be able to make use of this training program . . . am I gonna be able to make it through the twenty-six weeks of schooling, or possibly one year. These are the things that have bothered me which are important. I have no time for dates, you know, because I'm very busy trying to keep a roof over my head and provide three meals a day. It's one of the problems you face when you have to go from job to job and you never know when you are going to have a job and you never know what the outcome is going to be.

THE UNEMPLOYED: A SOCIAL-PSYCHOLOGICAL PORTRAIT

The long trail back! It was a journey without an horizon. There was nothing behind but defeat, and nothing ahead but emptiness. To the one side there was a desert of loneliness and to the other a morass of despair. There was nothing to look up to, and so my eyes remained downcast. I did not want to live, and yet I could not die. A flood of hot tears would have relieved the pent-up feeling deep within me, but I could not even cry. There was no relief of any sort, neither death nor tears, and because there was no escape I went blindly on, aware of the wind and cold, but impervious to them.

Earl Denman
ALONE TO EVEREST

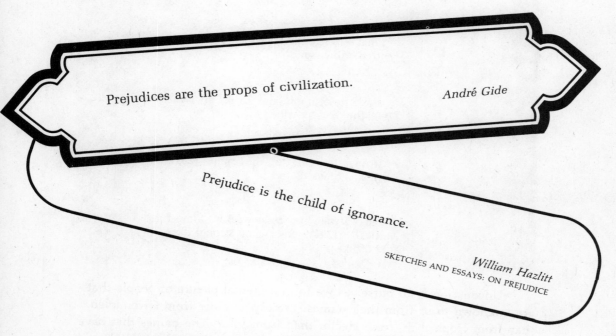

Prejudices are the props of civilization.

André Gide

Prejudice is the child of ignorance.

William Hazlitt
SKETCHES AND ESSAYS: ON PREJUDICE

One definition of prejudice is "an avertive or hostile attitude toward a person who belongs to a group, simply because he belongs to that group, and is therefore presumed to have the objectionable qualities ascribed to that group" (Gordon W. Allport).

Can you write your own definition of prejudice? Have you ever been prejudiced in your dealings with another? Have you ever been the victim of another's prejudice? Write about these experiences in your journal.

Very long final stroke (195): extravagant.

Final stroke rising (196): self-conscious, living in clouds, impractical.

Final stroke curls over (197): protective, having desire to shield others.

Final stroke rises to right (198): brave, daring, willing to take a chance.

Final stroke curls under (199): self-centred, rather selfish.

Weak descent of final stroke to right (200): timid, weak-willed.

Strong descent to the right (201): obstinate, quick tempered.

Final stroke descends weakly, almost vertically (202): possessing strong likes and dislikes.

Unconsciously to ourselves we form a mental picture of people that are unknown to us from their names. We expect more from Gwendolen than from Hephzibah, from Hector than from John. The names that have become famous are those which have a sonorous and stately ring, George Washington, Alexander Hamilton, Lafayette, Shakespeare, Wolfgang von Goethe, Gustavus Adolphus, Alfred Tennyson, Ludovico da Vinci, Michael Angelo Buonarrotti, Raffaelle Sanzio. One can understand how an obscure Corsican with such a name as Napoleon Bonaparte might have conquered the world.

William S. Walsh

158

Incident

Once riding in old Baltimore,
  Heart-filled, head-filled with glee,
I saw a Baltimorean
  Keep looking straight at me.

Now I was eight and very small,
  And he was no whit bigger,
And so I smiled, but he poked out
  His tongue and called me, "Nigger."

I saw the whole of Baltimore
  From May until December;
Of all the things that happened there
  That's all that I remember.

                    Countee Cullen

Walter Dumont and His Medal

As I saunter'd along the high road yesterday, I stopp'd to watch a man near by, ploughing a rough stony field with a yoke of oxen . . . . His name was Walter Dumont, a farmer, and son of a farmer, working for their living. Three years ago, when the steamer "Sunnyside" was wreck'd of a bitter icy night on the west bank here, Walter went out in his boat—was the first man on hand with assistance—made a way through the ice to shore, connected a line, perform'd work of first-class readiness, daring, danger, and saved numerous lives. Some weeks after, one evening when he was up at Esopus, among the usual loafing crowd at the country store and postoffice, there arrived the gift of an unexpected official gold medal for the quiet hero. The impromptu presentation was made to him on the spot, but he blush'd, hesitated as he took it and had nothing to say.

                    Walt Whitman
AUTOBIOGRAPHIA OR THE STORY OF A LIFE

159

Old Bert was at his best when telling his amazing stories of military prowess. He had fought on one side or the other, as an airman of course, in the Turkish-Bulgarian war of 1912. In the next breath he had been a Gor-bli-me Tommy fighting with Kitchener's Army when it was making its heroic stand during the Battle of Mons. Before his listeners could get a few facts substantiated, Bert had transferred to the French Foreign Legion and was taking credit for active service from August 1914 to December 1914. His tales were so credible, few of his listeners bothered to check his credentials.

Arch Whitehouse
HEROES AND LEGENDS OF WORLD WAR I

During the First Battle of the Marne, my uncle, Sergeant Arthur Whitehouse, who was manning one of the few machine guns allotted to his regiment, gallantly hung onto his post until he was the only man of his gun team left alive. Unquestionably, he fought well with outstanding valor and maintained the traditions of the Lancasters (The King's Own). One of his superior officers recommended him for the Victoria Cross, but another commissioned gentleman, who valued field tactics above the courage of one heroic soul, charged the sergeant with disclosing his company's position and demanded that he be court-martialed. Somewhere between these divergent viewpoints a happy medium was reached; my uncle was deprived of his sergeant's stripes, but given the Distinguished Conduct Medal—an award that could be bestowed on any regimental baker who had turned out his quota of loaves of bread during his particular period of wartime servitude.

Arch Whitehouse

With a firm step and a cheerful countenance, Sir Walter Raleigh walked across to the Cave House, where he was to prepare to die for being the enemy of Spain, under a sentence originally passed upon him for being Spain's friend.

Rafael Sabatini
HEROIC LIVES

Then the question arises, Why are beggars despised?—for they are despised, universally. I believe it is for the simple reason that they fail to earn a decent living. In practice nobody cares whether work is useful

160

or useless, productive or parasitic; the sole thing demanded is that it shall be profitable. In all the modern talk about energy, efficiency, social service and the rest of it, what meaning is there except "Get money, get it legally, and get a lot of it"? Money has become the grand test of virtue. By this test beggars fail, and for this they are despised. If one could earn even ten pounds a week at begging, it would become a respectable profession immediately. A beggar, looked at realistically, is simply a business man, getting his living, like other business men, in the way that comes to hand. He has not, more than most modern people, sold his honor; he has merely made the mistake of choosing a trade at which it is impossible to grow rich.

George Orwell
DOWN AND OUT IN PARIS AND LONDON

Once upon a time there lived a man whose one wish and prayer was to get rich. Day and night he thought of nothing else, and at last his prayers were granted, and he became very wealthy. Now being so rich, and having so much to lose, he felt that it would be a terrible thing to die and leave all his possessions behind; so he made up his mind to set out in search of a land where there was no death. He got ready for his journey, took leave of his wife, and started. Whenever he came to a new country the first question that he asked was whether people died in that land, and when he heard that they did, he set out again on his quest. At last he reached a country where he was told that the people did not even know the meaning of the word death. Our traveller was delighted when he heard this, and said:_____

_____

Andrew Lang
THE RED FAIRY BOOK

The Latest Decalogue

Thou shalt have one God only; who
Would be at the expense of two?
No graven images may be
Worshipped except currency.
Swear not at all; for, for thy curse
Thine enemy is none the worse.
At church on Sunday to attend
Will serve to keep the world thy friend.
Honor thy parents; that is, all
From whom advancement may befall.
Thou shalt not kill; but need'st not strive
Officiously to keep alive.
Do not adultery commit;
Advantage rarely comes of it.
Thou shalt not steal; an empty feat,
When it's so lucrative to cheat.
Bear not false witness; let the lie
Have time on its own wings to fly.
Thou shalt not covet, but tradition
Approves all forms of competition.

Arthur Hugh Clough

Thursday, October 4th

A violent rain storm on the pond. The pond is covered with little white thorns; springing up and down: the pond is bristling with leaping white thorns, like the thorns on a small porcupine; bristles; then black waves; cross it; black shudders; and the little water thorns are white; a helter skelter rain and the elms tossing it up and down; the pond overflowing on one side; lily leaves tugging; the red flower swimming about; one leaf flapping; then completely smooth for a moment; then prickled; thorns like glass; but leaping up and down incessantly; a rapid smirch of shadow. Now light from the sun; green and red; shiny; the pond a sage green; the grass brilliant green; red berries on the hedges; the cows very white; purple over Asheham.

A WRITER'S DIARY
BEING EXTRACTS FROM THE DIARY OF VIRGINIA WOOLF

Perhaps one of the things people like most about snapshots is that they freeze an instant of time and hold it for us to examine. Try creating word snapshots of the places you go, the things and people you see. Try to achieve the same effect of an instant frozen in time.

The cataract strong
Then plunges along,
Striking and raging
As if a war waging
Its caverns and rocks among;
Rising and leaping,
Sinking and creeping,
Swelling and sweeping,
Showering and springing,
Flying and flinging,
Writhing and ringing,
Eddying and whisking,
Spouting and frisking,
Turning and twisting,
Around and around
With endless rebound:
Smiting and fighting,
A sight to delight in;
Confounding, astounding,
Dizzying and deafening the ear with its sound.

Robert Southey

I've just been reflecting for two hours on my father's conduct toward me, being deplorably worn down by a strong attack of the slow fever I've had for more than seven months. I haven't been able to recover from it: first, because I didn't have the money to pay the doctor; in the second place, because, having my feet constantly in the water in this muddy city owing to lack of boots, and suffering in every way from the cold owing to lack of clothing and wood for the fire, it was useless and even harmful to wear down my body with remedies to get rid of an illness which poverty would have given me even if I hadn't had it already. . . .

163

Just calculate the effect of eight months of slow fever, fed by every possible misfortune, on a temperament which is already attacked by obstructions and weakness in the abdomen, and then come and tell me that my father isn't shortening my life!

Were it not for my studies, or rather the love of glory that has taken root in my breast in spite of him, I should have blown out my brains five or six times.

THE PRIVATE DIARIES OF STENDAHL

Drawing by McCallister; © 1971 The New Yorker Magazine, Inc.

This day I have been informed that I am to be banished the dwelling-house by night, and to sleep in an out-house by myself, to try if the family can get any rest when freed of my presence. I have peremptorily refused acquiescence, on which my master's brother struck me, and kicked me with his foot. My body being quite exhausted by suffering, I am grown weak and feeble both in mind and bodily frame, and actually unable to resent any insult or injury. I am the child of earthly misery and despair, if ever there was one existent. My master is still my friend; but there are so many masters here, and every one of them alike harsh to me, that I wish myself in my grave every hour of the day. If I am driven from the family sanctuary by night, I know I shall be torn in pieces before morning; and then who will deign or dare to gather up my mangled limbs, and give me honoured burial?

My last hour is arrived: I see my tormentor once more approaching me in this wild. Oh, that the earth would swallow me up, or the hill fall and cover me! Farewell for ever!

James Hogg
THE PRIVATE MEMOIRS AND CONFESSIONS OF A JUSTIFIED SINNER

Sorrow

Why does the thin grey strand
Floating up from the forgotten
Cigarette between my fingers,
Why does it trouble me?

Ah, you will understand;
When I carried my mother downstairs,
A few times only, at the beginning
Of her soft-foot malady.

I should find, for a reprimand
To my gaiety, a few long grey hairs
On the breast of my coat; and one by one
I watched them float up the dark chimney.

D. H. Lawrence

Describe a particular scene at different times of day. Be alert for surprises. Don't let your preconceptions about what you will find interfere with your observation. For example, you may expect the scene to be quiet early in the morning but discover that actually there is a good deal of activity going on.

There's the clip clop of horses on the sunhoneyed cobbles of the humming streets, hammering of horseshoes, gobble quack and cackle, tomtit twitter from the bird-ounced boughs, braying on Donkey Down. Bread is baking, pigs are grunting, chop goes the butcher, milk-churns bell, tills ring, sheep cough, dogs about, saws sing. Oh, the Spring whinny and morning moo from the clog-dancing farms, the gulls' gab and rabble on the boat-bobbing river and sea and the cockles bubbling in the sand, scamper of sanderlings, curlew cry, crow caw, pigeon coo, clock strike, bull bellow, and the ragged gabble of the beargarden school as the women scratch and babble in Mrs. Organ Morgan's general shop where everything is sold: custard, buckets, henna, rat-traps, shrimp-nets, sugar, stamps, confetti, paraffin, hatchets, whistles.

Dylan Thomas

The liveliest place in the house was the kitchen, which occupied half the basement. I had my breakfast there in the mornings: café au lait and whole-wheat bread. Through the window high in the wall you could see hens parading; guinea fowl, dogs, and sometimes human feet passed by. I liked the massive wood of the table, the benches and the chests and cupboards. The cast-iron cooking range threw out sparks and flames. The brasses shone: there were pots of all sizes, caldrons, skimming ladles, preserving pans and warming pans; I used to love the gaiety of the glazed dishes with their paintbox colors, the variety of bowls, cups, glasses, basins, porringers, celery dishes, pots, jugs, and pitchers. What quantities of cooking pots, frying pans, soup kettles, stew pans, cassolettes, soup tureens, platters, saucepans, pie tins, colanders, graters, choppers, mills, mincers, molds, and mortars—in cast iron, earthenware, stoneware, porcelain, aluminum and tin!

Simone de Beauvoir
MEMOIRS OF A DUTIFUL DAUGHTER

166

I too many and many a time cross'd the river of old, . . .
Saw the white sails of schooners and sloops, saw the ships at anchor,
The sailors at work in the rigging or out astride the spars,
The round masts, the swinging motion of the hulls, the slender
    serpentine pennants,
The large and small steamers in motion, the pilots in their pilot-houses,
The white wake left by the passage, the quick tremulous whirl of
    the wheels,
The flags of all nations, the falling of them at sunset,
The scallop-edged waves in the twilight, the ladled cups, the
    frolicsome crests and glistening,
The stretch afar growing dimmer and dimmer, the gray walls of the
    granite storehouses by the docks,
On the river the shadowy group, the big steam-tug closely flank'd on
    each side by the barges, the hay-boat, the belated lighter,
On the neighboring shore the fires from the foundry chimneys burning
    high and glaringly into the night,
Casting their flicker of black contrasted with wild red and yellow
    light over the tops of houses, and down into the clefts of
    streets.

Walt Whitman

Assume for the moment that the gentleman in the bowler hat . . . insists that he is the sole reality, while everything else appears only in his imagination. However, he cannot deny that his imaginary universe is populated with apparitions that are not unlike himself. Hence he has to grant them the privilege, that they themselves may insist that they are the sole reality and everything else is only a concoction of their imaginations. On the other hand, they cannot deny that their fantasies are populated by apparitions that are not unlike themselves, one of which may be *he,* the gentleman with the bowler hat.

SIGN, IMAGE, SYMBOL
Edited by Gyorgy Kepes

*Illustration used
by permission of
Gyorgy Kepes.*

Record some period of a day in as minute detail as you can. It might be a time when you're waiting for someone or something. It might be a boring day when it seems as if nothing is happening. Or you might deliberately choose a couple of hours and go to a street corner or construction site or just sit in your room. Keep your journal with you and try to record everything—everything you see, hear, smell, taste, and touch, everything you think, all your emotions.

What makes you believe that Ramses II, Charlemagne, Peter the Great, Elizabeth I, René Descartes, or Thomas Jefferson ever existed? What evidence do you have to show that an ancestor of yours was alive a thousand years ago?

Put yourself into a situation that allows you to write a fairly complete record of your attitudes now. Try this: go through a newspaper and jot down twenty headlines, more if the idea is especially appealing to you. Leave a line or two in your journal after each headline so that you can write down, in quick phrases, your reactions to each. This may make fascinating reading later on, even a few months from now.

Self-Portrait

I resemble everyone
but myself, and sometimes see
in shop-windows,
despite the well-known laws
of optics,
the portrait of a stranger,
date unknown,
often signed in a corner
by my father.

A. K. Ramanujan

Mirror

When you look	kool uoy nehW
into a mirror	rorrim a otni
it is not	ton si ti
yourself you see,	,ees uoy flesruoy
but a kind	dnik a tub
of apish error	rorre hsipa fo
posed in fearful	lufraef ni desop
symmetry.	.yrtemmys

John Updike

At Present Writing—Personal

May 31, '82.—"From to-day I enter upon my 64th year. The paralysis that first affected me nearly ten years ago, has since remain'd, with varying course—seems to have settled quietly down, and will probably continue. I easily tire, am very clumsy, cannot walk far; but my spirits are first-rate. I go around in public almost every day—now and then take long trips, by railroad or boat, hundreds of miles—live largely in the open air—am sunburnt and stout, (weigh 190)—keep up my activity and interest in life, people, progress, and the questions of the day. About two-thirds of the time I am quite comfortable. What mentality I ever had remains entirely unaffected; though physically I am a half paralytic, and likely to be so, long as I live. But the principal object of my life seems to have been accomplish'd—I have the most devoted and ardent of friends, and affectionate relatives—and of enemies I really make no account."

Walt Whitman
AUTOBIOGRAPHIA OR THE STORY OF A LIFE

Who is the oldest person you know? What can you learn from that person—from his or her life, successes, failures, pleasure, and pain—that would be valuable in leading your own life?

Find the tiniest object you can and, after studying it closely, describe its features fully. Use a magnifying glass or microscope, if available; what features not visible to the naked eye do they reveal?

little things
grow.
big things
eat
little things.
beauty
is here,
just
absorb it.
but don't
forget the
little things
which
make it
beautiful.
the
butterflies
are small,
they make the sky
beautiful.
don't forget
the
little things.

Rob LaPorte
JOURNAL

Little Things

Little things, that run, and quail,
And die, in silence and despair!

Little things, that fight, and fail,
And fall, on sea, and earth, and air!

All trapped and frightened little things,
The mouse, the coney, hear our prayer!

As we forgive those done to us,
—The lamb, the linnet, and the hare—

Forgive us all our trespasses,
Little creatures, everywhere!

James Stephens

Some examples of graffiti: actual statements written on the walls of . . .

a coffeehouse—

WE ARE THE PEOPLE OUR PARENTS WARNED US ABOUT.

a subway—

Chicken Little was right

Richard Hanser
[adapted slightly]

Use a page in your journal to write down examples of graffiti that you find and feel are particularly expressive. You might also use the same page to record some of your own creations.

Phizzog

This face you got,
This here phizzog you carry around,
You never picked it out for yourself, at all, at all—did you?
This here phizzog—somebody handed it to you—am I right?
Somebody said, "Here's yours, now go see what you can do with it."
Somebody slipped it to you and it was like a package marked:
"No goods exchanged after being taken away"—
This face you got.

Carl Sandburg

172

At 35, Paul Gauguin worked in a bank.
It is never too late.

Night school at the School of Visual Arts, 209 East 23rd Street.

If today were a meal, what would it be like?

Prune Pulp

Stew $\frac{1}{2}$ pound prunes in 2 cups of water until quite soft and then rub them through a coarse sieve. Put this pulp back in the water in which the prunes were cooked, add one teaspoon sugar and boil for about ten minutes.

THE SETTLEMENT COOK BOOK

To Pluck Wild Duck

$\frac{3}{8}$ lb. or $1\frac{1}{2}$ slabs paraffin   7 quarts boiling water
Melt paraffin in water. Dip duck in and out of boiling
Mixture 4 or 5 times. Cool from 3 to 5 minutes, or until paraffin
has coated feathers. Then pluck.

The Settlement Cook Book

Every inch of the room was covered with furniture. Chairs stood on couches that lay on tables; mirrors nearly the height of the door were propped, back to back, against the walls, reflecting and making endless the hills of desks and chairs with their legs in the air, sideboards, dressing tables, chests-of-drawers, more mirrors, empty bookcases, washbasins, clothes cupboards. There was a double bed, carefully made, with the ends of the sheets turned back, lying on top of a dining table on top of another table; there were electric lamps and lampshades, trays and vases, lavatory bowls and basins, heaped in the armchairs that stood on cupboards and tables and beds, touching the ceiling. The one window, looking out on the road, could just be seen through the curved legs of sideboards on their backs. The walls behind the standing mirrors were thick with pictures and picture frames.

Mr. Allingham climbed into the room over a stack of mattresses, then disappeared.

"Hop in, boy." His voice came up from behind a high kitchen dresser hung with carpets; and, climbing over, Samuel looked down to see him seated on a chair on a couch, leaning back comfortably, his elbow on the shoulder of a statue.

Dylan Thomas

Lord Byron's establishment consists, besides servants, of ten horses, eight enormous dogs, three monkeys, five cats, an eagle, a crow, and a falcon; and all these, except the horses, walk about the house . . . as if they were the masters of it . . . . After I have sealed my letter, I find that my enumeration . . . was defective . . . I have just met on the grand staircase five peacocks, two guinea hens, and an Egyptian crane.

Percy Bysshe Shelley
LETTER TO THOMAS LOVE PEACOCK

A lady was awoke in the night with the disagreeable sense of not being alone in the room, and soon felt a thud upon her bed. There was no doubt that some one was moving to and fro in the room, and that hands were constantly moving over her bed. She was so dreadfully frightened that at last she fainted. When she came to herself, it was broad daylight, and she found that the butler had walked in his sleep and had laid the table for fourteen upon her bed.

Augustus Hare
THE STORY OF MY LIFE

Once there was a whole lot of bird-seed around the room because an author had adopted a chicken. It was impossible to explain to anyone just why he had adopted the chicken, but still more impossible to know why he had bought the bird-seed for the chicken. The chicken was later broiled and the bird-seed thrown out, but the question of whether the man was an author or a lunatic was still unsolved in the minds of the hotel servants who had to deal with the situation. The hotel servants didn't understand it. They didn't understand how months later the author could write a story about it, but they all bought the magazine.

F. Scott Fitzgerald
NOTE-BOOKS

Compose a letter to someone you haven't seen in a long time—five to ten or more years. Read it over. What have you left out of your letter? Why? Do you think you might actually send it?

I'm not thinking of those X's and Y's
that just kind of stick to the page
in my Algebra book—I think you
have to read between the lines to
make anything of them.
All I see is that mountain out
there: big and cold with all the snow . . .
but there's something magnetic
about it; I want to climb it if
the snow is innocent and doesn't
turn into ice that cuts my bare feet.
And when I do, will you still be on
the other side?

Sue Hall
JOURNAL

I had begun to be very uneasy my dear Jane, on account of your long, long silence. I could not for a moment think you had forgotten me, no, Jane, I hope that will never be and that you will remember with affection your Friend Dorothy, but I feared that you had put off writing to me from day to day till at last you knew not how to begin, you seem to fear least I should be angry with you, angry! my dear Jane, how is that possible when you can so well account for your silence; I pity you from my heart; but hope in the next six weeks you will let me have twice the number of Letters you would have done, if you had not been so long unable to write. Oh Jane! how dearly do I love you! no words can paint my affection and friendship for you my dear Girl. When shall we meet! sometimes I am in despair and think that happy time will never arrive, at others I am all hope, but despair, alas! frequently gets the better of me.

Dorothy Wordsworth
LETTER TO JANE POLLARD

Friendship that lacks truth
is like a silver dandelion:
one sudden jagged move,
and it's gone with the wind.
But, where honesty
with each other
prevails,
mole-hill upon mole-hill
will eventually form
that mountain.

Sue Hall
JOURNAL

If you grow tired of writing constantly about yourself—your ideas, your experiences, your hopes, your reactions, your life—invent a character and begin writing about him or her—the life he or she has.

Choose someone you know and try to describe as completely as you can how his or her attitudes differ from yours.

I made it back to the Lex subway an jus in time for the rush. Train jammed to the doors with sweatin people comin home from work. It make me laugh inside to look at them. All of them so beat an worried an knocked out. They so tired lookin you could take any thing from them you wanted. Some of them all scrunched up in the cars tryen to read they newspapers.

I standen next to a PR readen a news paper written in Porto Rican. Front page have a picture of some dead people layin on the floor of a room an some big print in Porto Rican I guess it tellin you that they dead. I standen right up front in the first car up against the door so I can see the tunnel an far down the track you can see the stations comin tord you.

I like it up there in front. You get the feelin that you rushin thru the tunnel like a jet. Whooom! You put you head right up against the glass so you cant see nothin of the train an then you get the feelin they is nothin aroun you or under you but only speed. Come roarin thru an when I see the station comin I step down soft on the brake an bring it to a stop. Smooth Man.

Warren Miller
THE COOL WORLD

"What if . . . ?" is a question many writers, particularly writers of science fiction and fantasy, use to start them on the track of a new story. Try applying it to yourself. What if some enormous change occurred in your world? How would it change your life? How would it change you?

Write about your day as if it were a passage from a novel. Refer to yourself in the third person.

Exaggerate and elaborate as you wish—there's truth to be found in fiction too.

After each strike we moved in silence for a while, with only the tearing wind and slashing rain. Then the rocks would begin a shrill humming, each on a slightly different note. The humming grew louder and louder. You could feel a charge building up in your body. Our hair stood on end. The charge increased, and the humming swelled, until everything reached an unbearable climax. Then the lightning would strike again—with a crack like a gigantic rifle shot. The strike broke the tension. For a while we would grope forward in silence. Then the humming would begin again.

Frank W. Lane
THE ELEMENTS RAGE

"Give it up," said the Skipper, "and come with me."

With a sad smile I lifted my foot heavily and showed him what had me round the ankle. "Pooh," he said. "You could berth with the second mate. There's room there. I could sign you on as purser. You come."

I stared at him. The fellow meant it. I laughed at him.

"What," I asked conclusively, "shall I do about all this?" I waved my arm round Fleet Street, source of all the light I know, giver of my gift of income tax, limit of my perspective. How should I live when withdrawn from the smell of its ink, the urge of its machinery?

"That," he said. "Oh, dash that!"

H. M. Tomlinson
THE SEA AND THE JUNGLE

If today were a piece of music, what would it be like?

I had fallen in love with words. The first poems I knew were nursery rhymes, and before I could read them for myself I had come to love just the words of them, the words alone. What the words stood for, symbolized, or meant, was of very secondary importance; what mattered was the *sound* of them as I heard them for the first time on the lips of the remote and incomprehensible grown-ups who seemed, for some reason, to be living in my world. And these words were, to me, as the notes of bells, the sounds of musical instruments, the noises of wind, sea, and rain, the rattle of milkcarts, the clopping of hooves on cobbles, the fingering of branches on a window pane, might be to someone, deaf from birth, who has miraculously found his hearing. I did not care what the words said, overmuch, nor what happened to Jack & Jill & the Mother Goose rest of them; I cared for the shapes of sound that their names, and the words describing their actions, made in my ears; I cared for the colors the words cast on my eyes. I realize that I may be, as I think back all that way, romanticizing my reactions to the simple and beautiful words of those pure poems; but that is all I can honestly remember, however much time might have falsified my memory. I fell in love—that is the only expression I can think of—at once, and am still at the mercy of words, though sometimes now, knowing a little of their behavior very well, I think I can influence them slightly and have even learned to beat them now and then, which they appear to enjoy.

Dylan Thomas

. . . names present to us—of persons and of towns which they accustom us to regard as individual, as unique, like persons—a confused picture, which draws from the names, from the brightness or darkness of their sound, the colour in which it is uniformly painted, like one of those posters, entirely blue or entirely red, in which, on account of the limitations imposed by the process used in their reproduction, or by a whim on the designer's part, are blue and red not only the sky and the sea, but the ships and the church and the people in the streets.

Marcel Proust
A REMEMBRANCE OF THINGS PAST

Visit a place you haven't been in a long time—five to ten or more years ago, if possible. How is it different? How are you different?

The room I lived in was heavy ceilinged, perfectly square, with walls the color of chipped dry blood. Jules Weissman, a Jewish boy, had got the room for me. It's a room to sleep in, he said, or maybe to die in but God knows it wasn't meant to live in. Perhaps because the room was so hideous it had a fantastic array of light fixtures: one on the ceiling, one on the left wall, two on the right wall, and a lamp on the table beside my bed. My bed was in front of the window through which nothing ever blew but dust. It was a furnished room and they'd thrown enough stuff in it to furnish three rooms its size. Two easy chairs and a desk, the bed, the table, a straight-backed chair, a bookcase, a cardboard wardrobe; and my books and my suitcase, both unpacked; and my dirty clothes flung in a corner. It was the kind of room that defeated you. It had a fireplace, too, and a heavy marble mantelpiece, and a great gray mirror above the mantelpiece. It was hard to see anything in the mirror very clearly—which was perhaps just as well—and it would have been worth your life to have started a fire in the fireplace.

James Baldwin

Find some incident buried deep in your memory. We all remember far more than we can immediately recall, but if we concentrate on a particular time or place in our past we can often liberate a memory we didn't know was there. Are there any memory aids that would be helpful to you?

180

It must have been some time between the age of six and eight that I became an evildoer. Through this episode I was to learn another commandment: *Thou shalt fight back.* I was a well-loved child, being the first-born; but for some years I became, inexplicably, a criminal child. With a devilish cunning, the criminal child worked his mischief as if he wanted to avenge himself against the universe and even, what was most cruel, against those he loved. The precious pages of my father's scientific notes were found torn up. The milk, stored for supper in the cool of the window-ledge, was found dosed with salt. My mother's clothes were mysteriously burnt with matches or else slashed with scissors. Ink was surreptitiously spilt on newly-ironed linen. Objects disappeared without trace. Nobody could intercept the hands of the criminal child—my hands. I was harangued at length, I was admonished, I often saw my mother's eyes fill with tears; I was beaten too, and punished in a hundred ways, because my petty crimes were mad, exasperating, incomprehensible. I drank the salted milk, I denied everything (naturally), I melted into wretched promises, and then went to bed, in inconsolable grief, thinking of King Lear leaning on Cordelia. I became taciturn and introverted. Now and then the crimes would stop, and life would become bright, until the coming of another dark day which I had learnt to expect with a vigilant inner certainty. Eventually a time came when I acquired a sure foreknowledge of evil: I knew and felt inwardly, that my mother's pinafore would be dirtied or slit with scissors. I waited upon chastisement, and lived amid rebuke—and yet I used to play and climb trees as if evil had never existed.

Victor Serge
MEMOIRS OF A REVOLUTIONARY

Monday's child is fair of face,
Tuesday's child is full of grace,
Wednesday's child is full of woe,
Thursday's child has far to go,
Friday's child is loving and giving,
Saturday's child works hard for his living,
And the child that is born on the Sabbath day
Is bonny and blithe, and good and gay.

Anonymous

One of my favorite pranks was the catching of flies. I had a way of cupping my hand and with a swift movement scooping the victim. I'd wait till one lighted on a desk. I'd scoop it up and hold it, buzzing, in my fist. I rarely missed, I had grown so expert. Then I'd look to find someone, preferably a girl, who had not seen me do it. If the child happened to be looking the other way—that was perfect. I'd place my fist near her head and call her name. She'd face around—and I'd open my hand and out would buzz the fly, startling the poor child and scaring her half to death. All who had seen the mischief would laugh as loud as they dared.

Once, the teacher caught me with my fist doubled up. She asked what I had in it. I wouldn't tell her. She got angry and, with the entire class looking on, made me come to her desk. She bade me hold my hand before her and open it. I did so—and out buzzed the fly straight at her face. I had to stay after school and do much spelling in atonement for that.

Jean Toomer
EARTH BEING

What has gone on in the United States during the past two generations is full of lessons and warnings for the rest of the world. The American housewife of an earlier day was famous for her unremitting diligence. She not only cooked, washed and ironed; she also made shift to master such more complex arts as spinning, baking and brewing. Her expertness, perhaps, never reached a higher level, but at all events she made a gallant effort. But that was long, long ago, before the new enlightenment rescued her. Today, in her average incarnation, she is not only incompetent (a lack, as I have argued, rather beyond her control); she is also filled with the notion that a conscientious discharge of her few remaining duties is, in some vague way, discreditable and degrading.

H. L. Mencken
IN DEFENSE OF WOMEN

Dec 24 Friday

I want to go soon and live away by the pond, where I shall hear only the wind whispering among the reeds. It will be success if I shall have left myself behind. But my friends ask what I will do when I get there. Will it not be employment enough to watch the progress of the seasons?

The Journal of Henry David Thoreau

Of all ridiculous things the most ridiculous seems to me, to be busy—to be a man who is brisk about his food and his work. Therefore, whenever I see a fly settling, in the decisive moment, on the nose of such a person of affairs; or if he is spattered with mud from a carriage which drives past him in still greater haste; or the drawbridge opens up before him; or a tile falls down and knocks him dead, then I laugh heartily. And who, indeed, could help laughing? What, I wonder, do these busy folk get done?

Sören Kierkegaard

The situation at home is, if anything, worse. An unfortunate medium called television has been invented just in time to take up the slack that has developed since educators decided against the wisdom of giving homework. Left to his own devices throughout the late afternoon, and having been taught to pursue his natural instincts rather than to think, the child lounges about reading comic books or sprawls in a chair before the television set. If his intellectual tone is limp from lack of exercise anywhere, his body tone is no better. This creature is sponge from head to foot.

Walter Kerr

WELL, USUALLY I GET UP ABOUT EIGHT-THIRTY AND TAKE A SHOWER AND SHAVE AND THEN JUST WAIT AROUND UNTIL TIME TO GO TO THE BUS TO GO TO WORK. THEN I GO TO WORK, WORK ALL DAY AND THEN I GET OFF AT SEVEN O'CLOCK AND CATCH THE BUS BACK TO WHERE I LIVE. I GO IN AND TAKE ANOTHER SHOWER AND CLEAN UP AND THEN I JUST USUALLY LIE DOWN AND READ. I HARDLY DO ANYTHING ELSE--- REALLY NOT MUCH ELSE TO DO.

THE UNEMPLOYED: A SOCIAL-PSYCHOLOGICAL PORTRAIT

IDLE HANDS ARE THE DEVIL'S WORKSHOP

Observe a sunset. Notice how the setting sun produces color changes in the scene; make notes on the color changes you observe.

Feb. 10. —The first chirping, almost singing, of a bird to-day. Then I noticed a couple of honey-bees spirting and humming about the open window in the sun.

Feb. 11. —In the soft rose and pale gold of the declining light, this beautiful evening, I heard the first hum and preparation of awakening spring—very faint—whether in the earth or roots, or starting of insects, I know not—but it was audible, as I lean'd on a rail (I am down in my country quarters awhile,) and look'd long at the western horizon. Turning to the east, Sirius, as the shadows deepen'd, came forth in dazzling splendor. And great Orion; and a little to the northeast the Big Dipper, standing on end.

Walt Whitman
AUTOBIOGRAPHIA OR THE STORY OF A LIFE

Write some entries as if they were letters to people in your past. There's much catching up to do in such a letter. In fact, you may find that you're a stranger now, someone who must be introduced, explained, justified.

184

The last words of William Allingham:
I am seeing things that you know nothing of.

The last words of Ludwig Börne:
Pull back the drapes! I'd gladly see the sun . . . .
Flowers . . . Music.

The last words of Thomas Carlyle:
So this is death—well . . .

The last words of Stephen Decatur:
I am mortally wounded, I think.

The last words of Mahatma Gandhi:
Oh, God.

The last words of Victor Hugo:
Good-bye, Jeanne, good-bye.

The last words of Giacomo Leopardi:
I can't see you any more.

The last words of the Duc Anne de Montmorency:
Do you think a man who has known how to live honorably for eighty years does not know how to die for a quarter of an hour?

The last words of Alexander Pushkin:
Life is ended. It is difficult to breathe. I am choking.

The last words of Gertrude Stein:
What is the question? . . . What is the question? . . . If there is no question, there is no answer.

The last words of Elinor Wylie:
Is that all it is?

DICTIONARY OF LAST WORDS

I learned this, at least, by my experiment: that if one advances confidently in the direction of his dreams, and endeavors to live the life which he has imagined, he will meet with a success unexpected in common hours. He will put some things behind, will pass an invisible boundary; new, universal, and more liberal laws will begin to establish themselves around and within him; or the old laws be expanded, and interpreted in his favor in a more liberal sense, and he will live with the license of a higher order of beings. In proportion as he simplifies his life, the laws of the universe will appear less complex, and solitude will not be solitude, nor poverty poverty, nor weakness weakness. If you have built castles in the air, your work need not be lost; that is where they should be. Now put the foundations under them.

Henry David Thoreau
WALDEN

Apart from the pulling and hauling stands what I am,
Stands amused, complacent, compassionating, idle, unitary,
Looks down, is erect, or bends an arm on an impalpable certain rest,
Looking with side-curved head curious what will come next,
Both in and out of the game and watching and wondering at it.
Backward I see in my own days where I sweated through fog with
          linguists and contenders,
I have no mocking or arguments, I witness and wait.

Walt Whitman

March 24. Thursday. Those authors are successful who do not write down to others, but make their own taste and judgment their audience. By some strange infatuation we forget that we do not approve what yet we recommend to others. It is enough if I please myself with writing; I am then sure of an audience.

THE JOURNAL OF HENRY D. THOREAU

186

Down in the Woods, July 2d, 1882. —If I do it at all I must delay no longer. Incongruous and full of skips and jumps as is that huddle of diary-jottings, war-memoranda of 1862-'65. Nature-notes of 1877-'81, with Western and Canadian observations afterwards, all bundled up and tied by a big string, the resolution and indeed mandate comes to me this day, this hour,—(and what a day! what an hour just passing! the luxury of riant grass and blowing breeze, with all the shows of sun and sky and perfect temperature, never before so filling me, body and soul)—to go home, untie the bundle, reel out diary-scraps and memoranda, just as they are, large or small, one after another, into print-pages, . . . It will illustrate one phase of humanity anyhow; how few of life's days and hours (and they not by relative value or proportion, but by chance) are ever noted.

Walt Whitman

Saturday, March 20th

But what is to become of all these diaries, I asked myself yesterday. If I died, what would Leo make of them? He would be disinclined to burn them; he could not publish them. Well, he should make up a book from them, I think; and then burn the body. I daresay there is a little book in them; if the scraps and scratching were straightened out a little. God knows. This is dictated by a slight melancholia, which comes upon me sometimes now and makes me think I am old; I am ugly. I am repeating things. Yet, as far as I know, as a writer I am only now writing out my mind.

A WRITER'S DIARY
BEING EXTRACTS FROM THE DIARY OF VIRGINIA WOOLF

List the most important people, things, places, or ideas in your life.

Don't stop. This journal is only a beginning.

187

Art Credits

ABCDEFGH   07987654
PRINTED IN THE UNITED STATES OF AMERICA